Post-Borderlandia

Latinidad

Transnational Cultures in the United States

This series publishes books that deepen and expand our understanding of Latina/o populations, especially in the context of their transnational relationships within the Americas. Focusing on borders and boundary crossings, broadly conceived, the series is committed to publishing scholarship in history, film and media, literary and cultural studies, public policy, economics, sociology, and anthropology. Inspired by interdisciplinary approaches, methods, and theories developed out of the study of transborder lives, cultures, and experiences, titles enrich our understanding of transnational dynamics.

Matt Garcia, Series Editor, Professor of Latin American, Latino & Caribbean Studies, and History, Dartmouth College

For a list of titles in the series, see the last page of the book.

Post-Borderlandia

===========

Chicana Literature and
Gender Variant Critique

T. JACKIE CUEVAS

Rutgers University Press

New Brunswick, Camden, and Newark, New Jersey, and London

978-0-8135-9453-8
978-0-8135-9452-1
978-0-8135-9454-5

Cataloging-in-Publication data is available from the Library of Congress.

A British Cataloging-in-Publication record for this book
is available from the British Library.

⊗ The paper used in this publication meets the requirements of the American
National Standard for Information Sciences—Permanence of Paper
for Printed Library Materials, ANSI Z39.48–1992.

www.rutgersuniversitypress.org

Manufactured in the United States of America

For the antepasadas:

Minnie

Ana

And for the next generation:

Avital

Contents

Preface and Acknowledgments   ix

Introduction: Gender Variance and
the Post-Borderlands   1

1. Chicana Masculinities   27

2. Ambiguous Chicanx Bodies   56

3. Transing Chicanidad   77

4. Brokeback Rancho   100

Conclusion: From a Long Line of Marimachas   118

Notes   141

Bibliography   153

Index   165

Preface and Acknowledgments

The seedlings for this project emerged as poems the year Gloria E. Anzaldúa died and morphed into the scholarly version of my hopeful effort to do what she called "work that matters." Many pages of this book were written or revised while I stared out at the waves from my cherished spot on the Gulf of Mexico amid the laughing gulls, brown pelicans, roseate spoonbills, and Ridley sea turtles of Padre Island. The Gulf has always been there for me, through several degrees, through unexpected upheavals as well as joys.

During the making of this book, my altar grew increasingly crowded after the death of several dear friends, including several writer friends who had urged me to write more. Ana Sisnett, Raúl Salinas, Camile Pahwa, Chinwe Odeluga, Amy Young, Devin Zimmerman, Laura Padilla, and Maggie Jochild left indelible marks. And my colleagues Cynthia Hawkins and Catherine Kasper will be missed. Ana Sisnett, in particular, would have relished holding this book in her hands and telling me why it matters.

Ana would have keenly understood how it was not merely my engagement with literature and queer theory but also my own engagement with gender variance that certainly informs this work. Like my own gender journey, this book has had many iterations and transformations. Perhaps this book grew from being a curious tomboy to a studious girly teen to a well-meaning young butch to a genderqueer butch Xicanx academic with an extensive collection of guayaberas and wingtips.

During the course of writing this book, shifting terms and times have made it challenging to attend to the many nuances and neologisms of LGBTQ+ vernacular. Some of the terms used in this book did not exist or were not in wide circulation when I first began the initial research. Indeed, innovative new terms, concepts, and movements may emerge before the ink dries, and that is part of the excitement of this work.

Throughout this process I have been particularly thankful for the activist and community spaces I have been able to call home deep in the heart of Texas, especially allgo, a statewide queer people of color organization. All the folks at the queer bailes, protests, vigils, committee meetings, workshops, fund-raisers, and tamaladas over the years have taught me what it means to make space for and to fight for vibrant queer and transgender people of color lives. It was through allgo that I have met many cherished mentors and long-term members of my queer familia. In particular, Sharon Bridgforth's insightful guidance and loving friendship have shaped my commitment to writing and working in community.

I am deeply grateful to the amazing writers and artists whose work I discuss in this book. Many of them generously shared their time and wisdom, including Adelina Anthony, Helena María Viramontes, and Deb Esquenazi. Helena graciously visited my Latina feminist theories class at Syracuse University, and Deb invited me to participate in a screening and talkback to discuss her film at her San Antonio premiere of *Southwest of Salem*.

Along the way, I have been able to share this work as it has developed in various venues, including conferences and journals. A version of chapter 2 first appeared in *Latino Studies* 12.1 (2014). A portion of chapter 3 was previously published in *Revue LISA* 21.2 (2013) in a special issue titled *Latinotopia*, edited by Francisco Lomelí and Karen Ikas.

My sincere gratitude must be expressed to dear colleagues and friends who have provided intellectual companionship, feminist collaboration, and tireless support—in particular, Chandra Talpade Mohanty, Alison Kafer, Sonia Saldívar-Hull, and Norma Cantú. A special thanks goes to my dissertation committee, including Domino Renee Perez, Ann Cvetkovich, Deborah Paredez, Jose Limón, Matt Richardson, and Lisa Lynne Moore.

Ricky T. Rodríguez must be thanked for his helpful feedback on this project; his suggestions were on point, and his work continues to inspire my own.

Numerous librarians and archivists were quite helpful in locating materials. Christian Kelleher, Carla Alvarez, and several others helped me at the Benson Latin American Collection at the University of Texas Libraries. A special thanks goes out to AnaLouise Keating of the Gloria E. Anzaldúa Literary Trust for helping me with materials from the Anzaldúa archive. Tom Kreneck and other folks were quite welcoming at the Mary and Jeff Bell Library Special Collections and Archives at Texas A&M University at Corpus Christi.

I developed some of the ideas for this project during my time as a faculty member at Syracuse University. At Syracuse, I had the good fortune to be surrounded and supported by amazing colleagues in women's and gender studies, including Chandra Talpade Mohanty, Minnie Bruce Pratt, Himika Bhattacharya, Dana Olwan, Gwen Pough, Vivian May, Robin Riley, Carolina Vargas, Bekki Orr, Soumitree Gupta, Kwame Otu, and Gohar Siddiqui. The Democratizing Knowledge collective, including Linda Carty, Paula Johnson, Silvio Torres-Saillant, Jackie Orr, Hayley Cavino, Sari Biklen, and others, made my time at Syracuse particularly engaging by providing a much-needed space for collaborating with local community partners and working toward democratizing the academy. Fabulous Syracuse neighbors welcomed my family and me into the university neighborhood. I am deeply grateful for the lovely Shabbat dinners hosted by Julie Gozan and Tom Keck and their family. Gladys McCormick connected me with colleagues and helped me find Mexican food. Sheru and Michael showed me how to use a roof rake to fight off the interminable snow.

I am grateful as well to my colleagues at the University of Texas at San Antonio who have supported my work along the way. Professor Sonja Lanehart, Brackenridge Endowed Chair of Literature and the Humanities, generously sponsored my participation in the National Center for Faculty Development and Diversity (NCFDD) program, which was instrumental in my finishing this book. My NCFDD small group members, Jessica, Danielle, Rima, and our coach Ray, provided pivotal support and encouragement.

The jota editorial crew—Anel Flores, Rita Urquijo-Ruiz, and Candace Lopez—kept me engaged in invigorating creative endeavors during this scholarly project. As a member of Macondo, I continue to be grateful to the fabulous Macondo network, including Sandra Cisneros, Ire'ne Lara Silva, Alex Espinoza, John Phillip Santos, and many others. For help with tracking down details for the bibliography and notes, I am indebted to graduate research assistants Megan Nieto, Stephanie Schoellman, and Calvin Hoovestol. I am grateful to all of the students over the years who have made teaching a dynamic adventure where we can think together and challenge each other. I want to give a special shout-out to Risa Cantu, Mary Gonzalez, and Richie Giddens.

I cherish the memories of camaraderie shared at many late-night writing binges at Clementine and other Austin coffee shops with Olga Herrera, Cristina Salinas, Virginia Raymond, María Cruz, and others. Erin Hurt and Hala Herby made our dissertation writing group a pleasure. Elvira Prieto, Crystal Kurzen, and Verónica Martínez-Matsuda modeled a generosity of spirit for which I am appreciative.

I could not have survived without my comadre Brenda Sendejo. Brenda, fellow Tejana scholar and Athena extraordinaire, met me for countless writing sessions, walks, and coffee check-ins; she definitely helped me follow our Windsor Park Elementary school motto "use my time and intelligence wisely." Much love also goes out to Priscilla Hale, Rose Pulliam, Lorenzo Herrera y Lozano, Orlando Ramirez, Virginia Raymond, Tom Kolker, Ocelotl Mora (aka Jr.), Sheree Ross, Miramar Dichoso, Ixchel Rosal, Lisa Byrd, and the rest of the extensive comadrazgo, queer kin, and loved ones who have helped me see this through. Lilia Rosas of Resistencia and Susan Post of Bookwoman deserve a special mention for continuing to keep the community-based bookstores alive and for hosting events where I could engage with some of the writers I write about in this book.

I do not take for granted my family's love and support. My three uncles—Sammy, Steve, and Mike—have always cheered me on and cheered me up. Their families have lovingly welcomed me and my own little familia. My in-laws, Roey and Jeff, have always been wonderfully understanding. I am thankful as well to Austin and the Medina cousins near and far.

I could never say enough to thank my mom, Cristina, whose grace under pressure, creativity, and humor are my guiding lights. Mama, I cherish your recent gift of the Star Wars bow tie, but I am especially grateful for your gift of telling me "You look handsome, mija." Thank you for unconditionally loving me in all my queer-gender variant ways.

The incomparable Jen Margulies, my spouse and coconspirator, surely knows, but I will tell her anyway, that she continues to amaze me with her stunning brilliance and capacious compassion that keep me keepin' on. Ever since that slow dance at the old-school dyke bar Port in the Storm in Baltimore, Jen continues to be my anchor. Avital literally cheered me on and set an example by writing five books in one week.

Because of all the aforementioned folks and all others who have lent their support, I have been able to complete this project. This book is an offering and a humble invitation to dialogue. I am grateful to all of the people who talked with me about my ideas along the way, and I look forward to the conversations to come.

Introduction

Gender Variance and the Post-Borderlands

In 1997 Elizabeth Ramirez, a Latina lesbian from San Antonio, Texas, went to prison for a crime she did not commit. Ramirez and four of her friends, all Latina lesbians, had been accused of gang raping two young girls—Ramirez's nieces—while Ramirez babysat them. During the trials of Ramirez and her peers, the prosecution brought forth a physician, Dr. Nancy Kellogg, as an expert witness. Upon examining the allegedly abused girls, Kellogg claimed to have noticed a supposedly abnormal mark on one of the children's genitalia, remarking in exam notes that "this could be satanic-related." Although the women's conflicting work schedules would have made it unlikely that they were even in the same place at the same time to perform the alleged ritualistic abuse, all four women were found guilty. Anna Vasquez, Kristie Mayhugh, Cassandra Rivera, and Elizabeth Ramirez received sentences ranging from fifteen to thirty-seven years (Barajas n.p.).

In 2010 the eldest of the accusers voluntarily recanted the accusation, explaining that her father had cajoled her and her sister into claiming that Ramirez and her friends had sexually abused them. Kellogg also recanted her expert testimony, admitting that it was based on "outdated" science. With the help of lawyers and volunteers from the Innocence Project of Texas and the Advocacy Project, the four women—dubbed the "San Antonio Four"—were released from prison in 2013 without being exonerated.

At a screening of *Southwest of Salem,* Deborah S. Esquenazi's documentary about their struggle, the San Antonio Four answered questions from the San Antonio public about their tabloid-worthy ordeal. Ramirez explained that she had rebuffed sexual advances from the young girls' father and that he may have orchestrated the accusations as retaliation against her. Although she had explained this to her attorney at the time, this evidence apparently was not taken seriously. She also mentioned that one of the jurors was a preacher who publicly claimed during their trial that "homosexuality is a sin," yet he was allowed to remain on the jury. An audience member asked whether the women thought they were treated so harshly by the criminal justice system because they are lesbians or because they are Latina. Anna Vasquez immediately responded "Both."

Vasquez's response echoes the claim put forth by Chicana lesbian writer Carla Trujillo. In the chapter "Chicana Lesbians: Fear and Loathing in the Chicano Community" in *Chicana Lesbians: The Girls Our Mothers Warned Us About,* Trujillo contends that "[t]he vast majority of Chicano heterosexuals perceive Chicana lesbians as a threat to the community." She attributes this "heterosexist response" to homophobia and goes on to say that "Chicana lesbians are perceived as a greater threat to the Chicano community because their existence disrupts the established order of male dominance, and raises the consciousness of many Chicana women regarding their own independence and control" (186). The San Antonio Four's experience stands as a stark example of the collision between racism and homophobia that targets Chicana lesbians and queer people of color for multiple transgressions of the social hierarchies that undergird U.S. culture.

While Trujillo's observation speaks to racialized sexuality as well as gender, Trujillo makes the connection between sexuality and gender specifically in regard to lesbian Chicanas as women. We can build on her formulation to account for a more expansive view of gender, particularly gender nonconformity. Certainly, gender nonconformity—especially in conjunction with sexual nonconformity—reveals the fissures in a seemingly coherent gender system that has been naturalized over time. In the case of the San Antonio Four, we can only imagine what their gender liminality or nonconformity may have contributed to how Ramirez and her counterparts were treated by agents of the justice system. According to Vasquez, their lawyers told them to wear dresses to appear more feminine—and presumably heterosexual and non-threatening—to the jury. The prosecuting attorney asked Ramirez on the stand whether she had a "gay relationship" with her friends, to which she replied that they were all just friends (Chammah n.p.). The litigators certainly understood that regardless of whether the accused identified as nonheterosexual and whether they had engaged in nonnormative sexual practices, their visuality as intelligible "women" could potentially hold sway over an audience looking for deviance as a supposed clue to morality. As Elvia Mendoza points out, prosecutors attempted to construct "another type of gender" (77) that would come to render them culpable in the eyes of the selected biased jurors. Undoubtedly, historical examples abound of stereotypes of the "mannish lesbian" being used to target nonnormatively gendered women as perverse threats to communal well-being. Fear of queer sexuality can bring out the homophobic sexuality police, but gender nonconformity can disrupt the social order by bringing one's ontological status as a categorizable human being into question.

Gender ambiguity can render a person illegible to community and loved ones—a "that" whom others attempt to assign to one side or the other of the dominant binary. For example, Felicia Luna Lemus's novel *Trace Elements of Random Tea Parties* illustrates the disruptive effect that gender nonconformity can have. When the "chicana dyke" (5) protagonist Leti dons men's clothing, her grandmother reacts in shock at her appearance by exclaiming, "Dear Mother of God. Is that a boy or a girl?" (167). Here, Leti's gender ambiguity renders her illegible to the grandmother, who refers to Leti as "that" and demands to know on which side of the dominant girl/boy binary Leti should be placed. In narratives such as Lemus's, it is not necessarily queer sexualities but rather queer genders that threaten a Chicanx[1] cultural or familial sense of unity.[2]

FIGURE 1. Still image from the film *Southwest of Salem* by Deborah S. Esquenazi.

In the case of the San Antonio Four, gender nonconformity haunted the whole ordeal but seems to have remained an unspoken question in the formal proceedings. In the footage shown at the screening of *Southwest of Salem*, one of the women sports a sleeveless T-shirt and a mullet, while another wears khaki pants, a wallet chain, and work boots. The masculine-appearing woman holds another woman in a tender embrace (Figure 1). Several of the women involved present themselves in ways that do not necessarily conform to heteronormative[3] gendered expectations, or cis-heteronormativity.[4] Their gender presentation brings up several questions. What effect does gender presentation have on understandings of sexuality and sexual identity? How does gender presentation relate to gender identity, particularly for gender-nonconforming individuals? How might we undertake a gender critique without assuming that subjects fit neatly on one side or the other of the dominant female/male sex and feminine/masculine gender binaries?

Post-Borderlandia takes up such questions. Using a gender variant critique, the book makes gender nonconformity an explicit question in order to understand its relation to queer sexuality and Chicanx identities, experiences, and representations.

Post-Borderlandia turns to literary cultural productions to ponder how Chicana authors have grappled with queerness as a locus of cultural tension, how gender and queer relate in the fictive worlds of gender transgressive and gender variant Chicanxs. As queer theorist José Esteban Muñoz observes in *Cruising Utopia*, "Turning to the aesthetic in the case of queerness is nothing like an escape from the social realm, insofar as queer aesthetics map future social relations" (1). By moving beyond a sole focus on sexuality or sexual orientation, I take seriously the ongoing commitment of the feminism of women of color to demand attention to the intersectional relationality among multiple analytic categories such as gender, sexuality, race, and class and their material effects on embodied identities and practices.

Resisting a strict adherence to the sex/gender binaries, Lemus and other authors in this study have opened up a space for expanding how Chicana cultural productions have addressed questions of gender conformity, particularly in relation to lesbian and other queer sexualities and identities. They complicate gendered representations and critiques by amplifying the category of gender. They prompt us to ask questions not just about sexuality or gender but also about both in tandem. What do Chicana lesbians and gender-nonconforming queers threaten? How do they threaten the dominant heteropatriarchal gender system that governs normative Chicano communities? How are gender nonnormative subjects targeted as transgressors of the gender binary? Is it, as E. J. Graff remarks, "for the sex they have," or "for the sex they appear to be" (n.p.)? How far out of bounds does one have to be in order to be perceived as a sexual outlaw versus (or in addition to) a gender outlaw? And how do gender and sexuality relate, particularly for racialized and otherwise minoritized subjects?

Focusing on Chicana texts whose characters transgress the gender binary—the suit-donning Chicana butch, the ambiguously gendered brown body, the excessively feminine queer, the transgender Chicanx person—*Post-Borderlandia* argues that gender nonconformity has shaped understandings of queerness. Through careful readings of Chicana texts, I show how representations of nonnormative genders have played a significant role in shaping queer Chicana literature. This project reexamines the archive of queer Chicana literature to include not only sexual difference but also gender variance.[5]

A queer Latina death ignited this project. In 2004, I had left my public school teaching job and was waiting to begin graduate school that fall. I received the news as it spread across the Internet: Gloria Anzaldúa had died. The author of *Borderlands/ La Frontera: The New Mestiza*, the editor of *Making Face, Making Soul/Haciendo Caras*, and Cherríe Moraga's coeditor of *This Bridge Called My Back: Writings by Radical Women of Color* had left an indelible mark on so many lives and minds. Concentric waves of mourning radiated out from her family, intimates, close friends, longtime colleagues, editors, comadres, readers, and fans. The grief from those who had never even met her seemed palpable as well. For many, the loss of Anzaldúa, theorist of Chicana borderlands transcendence, marked the end of an era.

What struck me especially hard about her death was that Anzaldúa had been in the final stages of writing her dissertation. She died ABD, all but dissertation.[6] As a first-generation college student, I had been deeply inspired by Anzaldúa's writing, and upon her death I vowed that I would do everything in my power to become one of the fewer than one percent of Latinas to earn a doctorate. When I started graduate school, groups of community activists and university constituents began working together to plan a tribute event to memorialize Anzaldúa, and I joined that effort via my involvement with allgo[7] as well as through my new affiliation as a graduate student with the Center for Mexican American Studies at the University of Texas at Austin. Working with others to help organize the Austin tribute in Anzaldúa's honor helped many of us work through our collective mourning (Figure 2).

At the Austin tribute, Cherríe Moraga spoke as someone who had worked alongside Anzaldúa as a fellow activist and writer. Addressing the crowd of several hundred people, Moraga talked about how Anzaldúa had inspired a generation of Chicana

FIGURE 2. Poster announcing the 2004 Austin tribute in memory of Gloria E. Anzaldúa. Nettie Lee Benson Latin American Collection, University of Texas Libraries, University of Texas at Austin. Photo second from top, left side, *Gloria Anzaldúa at Disneyland, Late 1970s* by Randy P. Conner, PhD.

lesbianas to speak out against multiple oppressions. Moraga went on to say that Anzaldúa's writing would continue to move people to action but that other writers from the new generation of Chicana lesbians needed to take up Anzaldúa's charge to build alliances across race, gender, sexuality, and class. Moraga asked, "Who's next? Who will continue the work so that Gloria and I will not be the last generation?"

Like Moraga, Anzaldúa was deeply invested in imagining or reimagining a future for queer Chicanxs. In Anzaldúa's vision of the "new mestiza" in *Borderlands/La Frontera*, similar anxieties and ambivalence about the future seem to be at work, as is an idealistic hope for liberation via the development of a new individual and communal consciousness. As many of the attendants at the Anzaldúa public tribute testified, Anzaldúa's *Borderlands/La Frontera*, now in its fourth edition from San Francisco–based Aunt Lute Books, has become something of a classic. I cannot count how many people, especially undergraduates, have told me stories of becoming feminists, realizing their alliances to others across race, or coming out to their families after reading Anzaldúa or taking a women's studies class in which they were exposed to her work. Queer or not, so many young people I have worked with, when encountering Anzaldúa's *Borderlands/La Frontera* for the first time, experience what Anzaldúa termed the "Coatlicue state,"[8] an opening of consciousness. There are now conferences centered solely on her scholarship, and there is an organization called Society for the Study of Gloria Anzaldúa (SSGA) started by Norma Cántu and colleagues in 2005.

In South Texas, Anzaldúa's homeland in the U.S.-Mexican border region, the Gloria Anzaldúa Legacy Project distributes printed quotes by Anzaldúa in leaflet form at various community sites, such as women's centers. And her work is now widely anthologized in readers used in women's and gender studies, ethnic studies, and literature courses. Many people I encountered at the 2009 SSGA conference in San Antonio reported that learning about Anzaldúa's concepts such as "mestiza consciousness" shifted their sense of their experience as divided selves, people of color trying to survive in an Anglo-dominated United States. What their stories have in common is the struggle of feeling cut down the middle by a border within their consciousness and the potential for theorizing ways to harness that into a facultad they could use to skillfully rework the cultural clash they felt within and around them. For some, seeing Anzaldúa's work embraced by audiences beyond Chicanas created a space in which they could imagine themselves as welcome within a larger women's movement as well as within the Anglo-dominated academy.

Anzaldúan borderlands theory has been deployed as a critical lens for a multitude of marginalized experiences and cultures beyond the Chicana, Tejana, queer, feminist, academic, creative writer, activist position from which Anzaldúa developed her approach to understanding a mestiza, or mixed-race, experience along the border. Anzaldúa's border is both the physical borderlands where Mexico meets the U.S. boundary and the resulting hybrid, dynamic consciousness required of borderlands subjects. When Anzaldúa says in *Borderlands/La Frontera* that "[t]he U.S.-Mexican border *es una herida abierta* [is an open wound] where the Third World grates against the first and bleeds" (25), she refers to the harsh border conditions such as the impoverished colonias where maquiladora workers live in shacks without running water while the U.S.-based corporations profit from their exploited labor. Anzaldúa refuses to discount those violences and the real affects and effects of the lived experience along the border, where "before a scab forms it hemorrhages again, the lifeblood of two worlds merging to form a third country—a border culture." Yet, beyond the actually existing border, Anzaldúa is also talking about a revolution of the mind, the psychic borderlands, where the mestiza and queer must contend with the normalized daily violence and trauma of racism, sexism, and homophobia.

Moraga's question—"Who's next?"—prompted me to investigate post-Anzaldúan authors and texts that have emerged to continue shaping queer Chicana literature. In my initial gathering of texts to consider, I was drawn to the fiction of Felicia Luna Lemus. Lemus's novel *Like Son* features a transgender protagonist and may be the first Chicanx novel to do so. Her work shares some concerns with Anzaldúa and Moraga's generation, such as challenging normative constructions of Chicano identity that render queerness outside of Chicanidad. But Lemus's venturing into genderqueer and transgender representations situates her work as working against some of the impasses in Moraga's and Anzaldúa's works, which have tended to rely on the concept of *mujer*/woman to shore up a coherent Chicana lesbian feminist subject. Just as Moraga's and Anzaldúa's writing works against a masculinist Chicano cultural nationalism and an Anglo-centric feminism, texts such as Lemus's fiction work against fixed notions of Chicana womanhood and normative gendered experience.

Lemus's work, with its genderqueer and transgender Chicanx characters, moves us beyond a borderlands mind-set in which borders can be transcended through a heightened state of consciousness whereby Chicanas can transcend conflicting Mexican and Anglo cultures that compete for their allegiance. Taking aim at the sex/gender binaries, Lemus negotiates a different set of borders than envisioned by Anzaldúa's theory of the borderlands.[9] Working in the post-borderlands, Lemus pivots away from a gender normative paradigm toward a more radical notion of gender by deploying a process of what José Esteban Muñoz, after Michel Pêcheux and Norma Alarcón, calls "disidentification." Muñoz characterizes disidentification as "a performative mode of tactical recognition that various minoritarian subjects employ in an effort to resist the oppressive and normalizing discourse of dominant ideology" (*Disidentifications* 97). Reading Lemus in this context opens up a way to engage with contemporary queer Chicana texts on their own terms, which includes but is not limited to an engagement with the Chicana lesbiana texts of the previous generation. Drawing on Muñoz, I read contemporary Chicana lesbiana texts that queer not only sexuality but also gender, such as Lemus's novels, as engaging in a complex process of disidentifying both with representations of white lesbianism as well as with heteronormative Chicanidad.

Disidentification refers to the process of manipulating dominant markings of the racialized queer subject in order to distance oneself from the oppressively dominant systems of representation. In this process, the minoritized subject critiques or disavows dominant representations in order to point out their absurdity or harmfulness. Building on Muñoz's work, I contend that it is not merely racialized sexuality but also the queering of gender that becomes a site for disidentification to be played out and explored in post-borderlands texts. In Lemus's narratives, for example, characters are identified as being Chicana, but they reconfigure dominant tropes of that category through the performance of queer or nonnormative genders. In the post-borderlands world, characters may be suggested to be Chicana but do not necessarily struggle with what that may mean to them. They are also queer but do not necessarily struggle much with that either. Their struggles tend to coalesce around issues of nonnormative gender expression or gender identity; they thus disidentify with Chicanidad and queerness through resignifying the relation between the two at the intersection of gender variance and genderqueerness.[10]

Muñoz critiques Anzaldúa, calling into question her formulation of the border-crossing mestiza, especially the queer mestiza, as the "supreme crosser of cultures." As Muñoz aptly points out, Anzaldúa's view "contains the potential for being too celebratory of queer diversity, and in doing so elides the recalcitrant racisms and phobias that are still present throughout queer culture" (*Disidentifications* 138). By claiming that the new mestiza consciousness can transcend its double bind of being on the border between two cultures through a "tolerance for ambiguity," Anzaldúa's borderlands theory does not fully recognize the power differential between dominant and subjugated cultures or assumes that it is easily possible to transcend said power differential through individual agency, the individual act of combining aspects of two opposing cultures.

Muñoz's theory of disidentification allows for the mestiza subject not just to tolerate ambiguity but also to incorporate it, messiness and all, into her identity. Thus, disidentification recognizes the complex circulation of power and its effects. It also acknowledges that the marginalized subject makes choices, enacting some degree of agency around what aspects of the dominant culture to identify with or against which to dis-identify. The performance of Chicana queerness and gender variance through disidentification scramble the codes of gender and sexuality, queering not just sexuality but also gender. One's gender expression might be expressed and queered along a complexly shifting continuum of possible femininities and masculinities and beyond. Thus, we can take a revitalized expansion of Anzaldúa's "tolerance for ambiguity" into a post-borderlandia.

In this process, integral strategies are irreverence and a bold disregard for in-group conventions, along with the simultaneous rewriting of those conventions. Such rewriting takes into account the intersection of gender and sexuality and, in particular, gender identity, gender presentation, and the myriad complexities associated with them. Muñoz describes such a process as a type of "revisionary identification" (*Disidentifications* 26), and I would modify this by suggesting that the process involves a queering of identification. Muñoz understands his work to be carrying on the legacy of *This Bridge Called My Back* and characterizes his work, then, to be "post-Bridge" (22); Norma Alarcón uses the term "post-Bridge" as well in her article "The Theoretical Subject(s) of *This Bridge Called My Back* and Anglo-American Feminism." Likewise, I consider my own project to be post-Bridge as well as post-Borderlands/ post-borderlands.

A post-borderlands project makes borderlands theory an explicit object of study, testing and pushing the limits of how borderlands theory has become so infused in Chicana studies as to become a default way of seeing, deployed as a nearly automatic lens.[11] It looks for the places where borderlands theory does not quite fit or hold, where it may be helpful yet not enough. One of those significant fissures is around the nonnormatively gendered queer body that the selected texts put at the center of their narratives. Post-borderlands is enunciated via an interplay between gender and sexuality under the sign of Chicanx gender variance. The texts that I have selected for the study negotiate race, nation, class, sexuality, and gender as shifting aspects of identity that coconstitute or intertwine inextricably in queer Chicanx subjectivities. In other words, these multiple aspects interact with and problematize what it means to be Chicanx. What interests me is how such subjects become constructed at the shifting nexus of multiple matrices of power and agency. These queer Chicanx cultural productions provide insight into how a subject becomes racialized, sexualized, gendered, and otherized in a U.S. context.[12]

These post-borderlands cartographies, such as Felicia Luna Lemus's fiction and Adelina Anthony's solo performances, engage in a combination of narrative and cultural strategies. Typically, they foreground the queer and/or gender variant subject through queer and/or gender variant characters, plots, contexts, and/or themes. Like many Chicanx cultural productions, these post-borderlands texts draw on both the real U.S.-Mexican border as a geopolitical site of contention and the metaphor of a border/lands as a psychically troubling yet potentially liberating space. They extend this work further by interrogating the function of queerness and gender variance in the definition of what it means to be Chicanx.

In the post-borderlands, queer Chicanx subjectivity may be illegible to traditional Chicanos and Mexicanos yet integral to the sustainability/survival of Chicanxs as a minoritized group in the hegemonic United States. Like many Chicanx literary texts, post-borderlands cultural productions displace the queer Chicanx. Unlike many Chicanx literary texts, however, they do not always attempt to recuperate traditional or nationalistic definitions of Chicanx. While borderlands and post-borderlands subjects have different ways of going about their cultural work, they each explore the queer subject's formation and, for some, the queer subject's contentious relationship to home and Chicanidad. In some cases that home is constituted by a homeland, a Chicanx community, the mythical Aztlán, an imagined future, or some combination thereof. For each of the narratives, gender variance plays a vital role.

Post-borderlandia is the site where gender variance pushes beyond the known frames of meaning and reformulates the potentialities of/for Chicanx. Post-borderlandia is where we participate in the processes of what Robin Wiegman calls "gender's endless critical pursuit" (100). In a post-borderlandia frame of mind, we keep open to the radical potentiality of queerness, of gender, of Chicanidades. In *Cruising Utopia*, José Esteban Muñoz distinguishes between possibility and potentiality: "Unlike a possibility, a thing that simply might happen, a potentiality is a certain mode of nonbeing that is eminent, a thing that is present but not actually existing in the present tense" (9). Muñoz argues that queerness is a "horizon" (19) and says that "queerness is not quite here" (21); it is a "not-yet-here" (29) that remains on the horizon as potentiality. We can amend his formulation to consider how gender variance dynamically relates to queerness, sexuality, race, and many other vectors, as gender variance and queerness often travel together. Post-borderlandia is where we find ourselves when Muñoz's not-yet-here suddenly rushes into being. Gender variant critique serves as an intervention in binaristic fixedness and suggests that there are myriad not-yet-here, as-of-yet imaginings for Chicanx gender(s) and for gender more broadly.

My work picks up where Catrióna Rueda Esquibel's *With Her Machete in Her Hand: Reading Chicana Lesbians* leaves off. Billed as "the first history of Chicana lesbian writing from the 1970s until today," the book offers the first book-length critical study of Chicana lesbian literature. Esquibel sets out "to map the terrain of Chicana lesbian fictions," which she defines as "drama, novels, short stories by Chicana/o authors that depict lesbian characters or lesbian desire" (1). In her readings of Chicana lesbian fictions, Esquibel examines how they represent various icons of Chicana femininity and sexuality, such as the Ixtacihuatl, La Llorona, and Sor Juana Inés de la Cruz. Esquibel performs close readings of texts that queer these traditional figures. Her study provides "a first full map" of Chicana lesbian literature and demonstrate how Chicana lesbian fictions are engaged in making community and making history. In articulating how Chicana lesbian fictions have taken on these figures from a queer perspective, Esquibel argues that much of Chicana lesbian literature has sought to document the existence of Chicana lesbians by creating histories through fictions. Building on Esquibel, my work maps a post-borderlands framework onto a body of Chicana lesbian literature in order to yield further insights into how these texts make Chicanx community and history, particularly by disrupting binaries.

This project is also influenced by Emma Pérez, whose *The Decolonial Imaginary: Writing Chicanas into History* levels a Chicana feminist critique of Michel Foucault. According to Pérez, "the decolonial imaginary" is a form of resistance to the colonial imaginary that has dominated the writing of histories. The decolonial imaginary can be described as the "interstitial space" (49) or the space within the "decolonial time lag" (14) where, for example, the colonized becomes the postcolonial or decolonized or the modern becomes the postmodern. The decolonial imaginary is that interstitial space in which one attempts to redefine a liberatory subjectivity beyond the limits of that imposed by the colonizer. Pérez's theory of the "decolonial imaginary" extends Gloria Anzaldúa's mestiza consciousness, a place where we can transcend the limits of traditional Western binaries, and Chela Sandoval's "differential consciousness," which "allows for a mobility of identities between and among various power bases" (xvi). The "decolonial imaginary" provides a stepping-stone for interpreting the transition occurring in this historical moment of the post-borderlands. Pérez's idea of a decolonial imaginary helps to locate the queer post-borderlands Chicanx subject somewhere between internal colonization and diaspora, in a psychosocial place full of potentiality. Overall, I contend that using this post-borderlands lens provides a productive way to read contemporary queer Chicanx texts by moving the critical conversation beyond the limiting debates of essentialist identity politics as well as the tried and trite notion of the borderlands as always liberating.

To this end, Yvonne Yarbro-Bejarano's innovative work in queer Chicanx studies calls for the dynamic use of multiple modes of analysis. In *The Wounded Heart: Writing on Cherríe Moraga* and in "Sexuality and Chicana/o Studies: Toward a Theoretical Paradigm for the Twenty-First Century," Yarbro-Bejarano argues that Chicana/o criticism must take into account multiple categories of analysis such as race, class, gender, and sexuality in order to avoid allowing one such mode to ignore or erase the concerns of another. In this study I try to maintain these concerns, particularly at the less explored intersection of race and ethnicity with queer gender and sexuality in contemporary Chicanx cultural productions, especially those that foreground queer subjects and their unreadable, transgressive subjectivities. Because of their concern with transgressions across socially imposed boundaries of identity and desire, such texts tend to explore how the queer Chicanx subject negotiates being in a contentious relationship to normatively situated Chicanx communities.

Building on Yarbro-Bejarano's work, Sandra K. Soto puts forth a critical approach she terms "reading Chican@ like a queer" as a way of reading racialized sexuality and displacing the race-based "monocausal paradigms" (121) that have historically dominated Chicano studies. As Soto notes, "Reading like a queer can be especially challenging when approaching noncanonical texts that are self-consciously produced through decisive and politicized efforts to contest systems of oppression and challenge the fixity of identity and that thus easily lend themselves to the intersectionality approach" (18–19). Soto points out that she "performs the first queer reading of Paredes's work" (13) and argues that in the prevailing scholarship on Paredes's foundational text *With His Pistol in His Hand,* "[t]he magnitude of that work and the masculine heroism it depicts have eclipsed . . . Paredes's own fiction and its subtle critiques of normative masculinity" (14). Soto's "reading Chican@ like a queer" reads against the grain of the heteronormative frameworks that have constricted the queer textures of Paredes's work and invites new interpretive possibilities.

Richard T. Rodríguez's work has offered a major contribution to queer Chicanx studies. His book *Next of Kin: The Family in Cultural Politics* "illustrate[s] how critical discourse on gender and sexuality allows us to critique the ways that Chicano/a cultural nationalism and notions of la familia continue to be codified by dominant articulations of masculinity" (20). Rodríguez's book reassesses the ways that queer sexuality and masculinities have shaped the Chicano movement and other texts and "serves as an interrogation of heteropatriarchal articulations of cultural nationalism by scrutinizing who and what counts as la familia" (2). As such, Rodríguez's approach informs the development of my gender variant critique that takes into account the ways queer gender nonconformity challenges hegemonic femininity and masculinity in Chicanx texts and contexts.

Several though not all of the writers in this study self-identify as Chicana and lesbian, queer, or transgender. I take a cue from Matt Richardson, who states in his book *The Queer Limit of Black Memory: Black Lesbian Literature and Irresolution* that "[i]t is Black women's vexed relationship to womanhood that has catalyzed Black lesbians to write most consistently about Black transgender experiences" (8). Likewise, I pay particular attention to the work of Chicana lesbians and queer authors because they have been at the forefront of urging reconsiderations of transgender and gender variant formations of gender and sexuality in Chicana literary and cultural productions.

While many of the cultural productions I analyze are by queer writers or about queer subjects, in order to explore unexpected relationships I also wish to engage normative texts that are either heteronormative or not usually considered queer. Ultimately, I am interested in not just the queer subject, queer author, or queer text but also how queerness contributes to an ongoing project of constituting Chicanx subjectivities. As such, my work seeks to analyze how contemporary Chicanx texts themselves theorize and figure queerness in Chicanx contexts.

Interrogating the tensions between Chicanidad and gender variance, the texts discussed in the project seek to claim destabilization and loss as productive sites of knowing and meaning for queer and gender variant people of color engaging in what theorist Roderick A. Ferguson in *Aberrations in Black* calls "queer of color critiques" in their daily lives and in their literary pursuits. Ferguson states that "queer of color analysis has to debunk the idea that race, class, gender, and sexuality are discrete formations, apparently insulated from one another" (4). Gender variant critique extends queer of color critique, built on the framework of women of color feminisms, to reconsider the relationships among gender, sexuality, race, and class, particularly when gender and intersecting categories become destabilized by gender variance.

Thinking through the lens of gender variance builds on the work of María Lugones. In "Heterosexualism and the Colonial/Modern Gender System," Lugones describes a "colonial gender system" that organizes women according to a hierarchy of racializations. She also poses the question "How do we understand heterosexuality not merely as normative but as consistently perverse when violently exercised across the colonial modern gender system so as to construct a worldwide system of power?" (187–88). While Lugones provides an understanding of how a Eurocentric colonial gender system persists in casting nonwhite women as nonwomen, her conceptualization of heterosexualism here does not fully account for queer sexualities and genders. Although Lugones speaks of a "multiplicity of genders," this multiplicity seems to be bounded by the category of woman, the very category that Lugones argues against as being restrictive. My approach here extends Lugones's concept of the "multiplicity of genders" to account for a broader array of possible genders, particularly as they relate to or inform understandings of queer sexualities and gender identities. This approach does not rely on projecting or assuming a "gynecratic" past or historical presence of a "third gender" in order to recognize the ways in which queer genders and gender variant expressions and identities expose the limitations of the gender binary system.

The methodological orientation of this project enacts what can be described as critical jotería studies. "Jotería" is a Chicanx term for queer people, and this culturally specific term captures the culturally specific focus and aims of the project.[13] The project stages a dialogue between Chicanx cultural studies and queer theory, domains that each have only somewhat recently begun to pay heed to the crucial contributions of the other. With this aim in mind, I draw on Juana María Rodríguez's commitment to deploying culturally specific terms that capture the nuances of practices, identities, and attitudes that comprise queer Latinidad. In her critical work, Rodríguez chooses culturally specific terms to denote Latinx queerness. In *Queer Latinidad,* explaining her preference for the terms "divas, atrevidas, and entendidas," Rodríguez asserts that these terms that "resonate with an attitude that steps beyond sexual practice or sexual identity into the realm of a politi-cized passion for liberation and empowerment" (24). As Rodríguez notes, "In Spanish, there is no direct translation for 'queer'" (24).[14] This linguistic gap due to nontranslatable language captures the unassimilable excesses of the unreadable, illegible, or ambiguously gendered bodies that stand at center stage in this project. Thus, I am not merely using "queer" as a simple umbrella term to try to be all-inclusive of a range of specific identities based on desire, sexual preference, identity, orientation, or sexual practice. Instead, I use "queer" to mean not just nonheterosexual sexuality but also non-normative gender expression. Additionally, I use it to signify the desire to disrupt normalized categories of social location.

Indeed, the term "queer" has a contentious history in some communities of color, including among Chicanxs. In her essay "To(o) Queer the Writer," Anzaldúa rejects the terms "lesbian" and "queer" for "representing an English-only dominant culture" (263). Instead, she chooses a Nahuatl term, patlache, to identify her love for other women.[15] Moving away from Anzaldúa in this regard, I have opted to use the language featured in the texts and cultural productions included in this study, many of which use the word "queer" or other terms such as "bucha" or "marica," which will be addressed later. Many of the contemporary cultural pro-ducers I discuss express increasing alignment with use of the term "queer." It can be said that the term "queer" is to "lesbiana" as the term "Chicano" is to "Mexican American." The latter is sometimes accused of being too mainstream or accommodationist, while the former is usually considered more politically oppositional or radi-cal. When the cultural producers specifically prefer a term such as "lesbiana" or "jota," I try to honor as much as possible their prefer-ences in self-naming. Thus, I use "queer" to signify an interpretive openness in my desire to remain attentive to the possibilities of Chicanx genderqueerness and various forms of gender variance.

"Chicanx" and "Latinx" are emergent terms in which the use of the "x" ending seeks to unsettle the gender binary bound up in terms such as "Chicano," "Chicana," and variations such as "Chicana/o" and "Chican@." The progression over time from "Chicana/o" to

"Chican@" to "Chicanx" suggests an ongoing desire to work toward more radically inclusive language. The slash in "Chicana/o" signaled a shift away from the masculine-centered construction of the word "Chicano" to bring the terms "Chicana" and "Chicano" into a hybridized term. Domino Renee Perez explains the term "Chican@" by saying that "[t]he 'a' ending, which indicates the feminine in Spanish, is at the center of a stylized 'o.' The circle used to form the 'o,' which in Spanish designates the masculine, is an extension of the 'a' but not separate from it" (210, note 6). Alicia Gaspar de Alba, in "Thirty Years of Chicana/Latina Lesbian Literary Production," says that the @ symbol suggests a "critical revision of gender as a category of analysis, as well as queer inclusivity" (471). The "x" in "Chicanx," "Latinx," and other terms attempts to move beyond the binary and offers a trans, genderqueer, gender nonconforming, and gender variant intervention that opens up the possibilities of ascribing any gender, or none at all, to the term. Macarena Gómez-Barris and Licia Fiol-Matta use the term "Latinx" "to signal a route out of gender binaries and normativities we can no longer rehearse. From the South and in the borderlands, the 'x' turns away from the dichotomous, toward a void, an unknown, a wrestling with plurality, vectors of multi-intentionality, and the transitional meanings of what has yet to be seen" (504). I use the terms "Chicanx" and "Latinx" throughout this book to open up such possibilities.[16]

The structure of this project moves from the most contemporary twenty-first-century representations of Chicana queerness, as in the plays of the Butchlalis and Adelina Anthony, back toward the 1930s fiction of Jovita González, whose work I read as an antecedent to Chicana lesbian feminist concerns of the late twentieth century. The fictional time imagined in these texts spans from the U.S. invasion of Mexico in 1846 to the 1960s and 1970s Chicano movement to the punk scene of the 1990s to the destruction of the World Trade Center towers on September 11, 2001. Significantly, these texts place the queer Chicanx at the center of those transformative historical moments. With this nonchronological approach, I begin with the most recent texts to engage with the questions of queer gender and sexuality taken up by this project in order to ascertain their contributions to queer Chicana literature.

The geographic and spatial locations of queer Chicanxs in the texts are as varied and shifting as the times represented. The settings shift from major urban Latinx centers to small rural towns. The Butchlalis and Adelina Anthony deal primarily with East Los Angeles as a site of queer Latina and Chicana experience, although Anthony hails from San Antonio and refers to various Texas cities in her recent work.[17] Jovita González's work, like Anzaldúa's, is deeply concerned with the South Texas region along the border between Mexico and the United States. Lemus's fiction takes us from Los Angeles to New York City, effectively shifting the center of gravity of traditionally canonical representations of Mexican Americans as being rooted in the U.S. Southwest. Lemus moves toward a more expansive Greater Mexico (a la Américo Paredes), depicting an even more amorphous and diffused diaspora of Mexican Americans across the full range of the U.S. landscape.

Generationally speaking, the Butchlalis and Adelina Anthony represent the current generation of Chicana and Latina queer writers, all born after 1970. They have been directly influenced by the previous generation of authors in that they have been mentored by Cherríe Moraga, with Anthony being trained by Moraga in the Stanford theater program. Lemus is also of this contemporary generation of writers, and her writing was first published in the late 1990s. Rocky Gámez is a writer whose short stories first appeared in print in the 1970s and 1980s; not much is known about her biography, but the first-person narrator of her short stories comes from and returns to the Rio Grande Valley of South Texas. Viramontes complicates an attempt to make a strict generational distinction among the authors, as she is a veteran of the Chicano movement like Anzaldúa and Moraga and remains on the forefront of innovative Chicanx literary production, pushing representations of Chicana queerness into new territory beyond even some of her queer authorial counterparts. González is the earliest of these writers (she died in 1983), and her 1930s fiction extends the history of Chicana lesbian feminist writing decades before the Chicano movement.

Traversing back and forth through time and place, the gender-queer and gender variant Chicanx characters in these texts certainly navigate some of the most persistent themes of Chicanx literature: home/land, familia, relationship to history, and loss. Nonetheless, the bringing together of these texts here is not meant to be a survey of representations of queer genders in Chicana literature. Rather, through such layering of history, place, and generation, the project keeps a kind of queer time, troubling what a generation is, troubling what lineage is. As Jack Halberstam asserts, "there is such a thing as 'queer time' and 'queer space'" (*In a Queer Time and Place* 1), and accounting for such queer time and place requires taking into account nonchronological and nonbiological accountings of time.

Tracking the figure of the gender variant subject, or what Halberstam calls "figurations of ambiguous embodiment" (17), across the Chicanx timescapes and landscapes of these texts, the project begins and ends in Texas. The project begins looking at the butch Chicana, then examines ambiguously gendered queer characters who destabilize the legibility of racial and ethnic categories, and ends by considering the effeminate man who resists his father's patriarchal and violent form of Mexican masculinity in favor of a queer artistic future.

The chapter "Chicana Masculinities" traces the figure of the butch in Chicana literature and performance. I begin by outlining the tendency in Chicana literature to use butchness or women's masculinity to signify lesbianness, beginning with the butch works of Cherríe Moraga and Rocky Gámez. These authors utilize the figures of the strong butch and the failed butch to expose the sexual and emotional vulnerability of Chicana borderlands butchness. After demonstrating how these fictional texts laid the groundwork for establishing the butch as a prominent Chicana queer figure, I examine how a new generation of Chicana writers and performance artists stage Chicana butchness. Through close readings of Adelina Anthony's "Mastering Sex and Tortillas" and the Butchlalis de Panochtitlan's *Barber of East L.A.*, I consider how this cadre of Chicana performers draws on and critiques traditional

Chicana butchness. This chapter discusses the tensions within representations of Chicana butchness. Moreover, it provokes a reconsideration of the tension and distance between Chicana butch representations and white feminist portrayals of lesbian gender.

The chapter "Ambiguous Chicanx Bodies" examines the queering of racialized gender through the use of gender ambiguity in *Their Dogs Came with Them*, a dystopic novel by Helena María Viramontes. Set in East Los Angeles during the Chicano movement, Viramontes's novel features a character named Turtle who is raised as a girl but lives as a young man on the streets, seeking to survive in a gang culture that values and depends on violent masculinities. Turtle's marginalized and unreadable body serves as both shelter and threat, and her possible queerness hovers as a ghostly possibility that seems inevitably lost. Viramontes uses the figure of the ambiguously gendered queer racial body to subvert the genre conventions of the queer coming-out narrative and the Chicanx coming-to-consciousness identity struggle, leaving her story as an emblem of disidentification.

The chapter "Transing Chicanidad" locates transgender Chicanxs crossing boundaries of gender and geography in twenty-first-century urban cityscapes. By transing[18] Chicanidad, Lemus asserts new subjectivities centered not around race/ethnicity or sexuality but instead around gender variance. Lemus's characters extend the geographic boundaries of Chicanidad from Los Angeles to New York. Her work also moves away from the borderlands struggles with mainstream white feminism and heteronormative Chicanidad toward the post-borderlands of genderqueerness and transgender embodiments, where it is not race or same-sex desire alone but also gender expression and gender identity that reconfigure notions of Chicanidad.

The chapter titled "Brokeback Rancho" recovers lost queer Chicanos in the early U.S./Mexican borderlands. Looking backward to earlier Mexican American letters, my queer reading of Jovita González's recovered 1930s novel *Caballero* reconfigures traditional Chicano and Latino literary histories by showing how this early writing used gender variance to critique Mexican and Anglo policing of boundaries against cross-racial and same-sex desire. I contend that it is not just race or class or gender or sexuality but rather gender variance that provides a mechanism through which González constructs an alternative affective queer history of the Mexican American borderlands that explores the fear of colonial domination, particularly through the feminization of culture and the expressions of nonheteronormative sexualities and genders. My queer reading of González's recovered fiction claims the author as a contributor to a queer Mexican American archive and demonstrates how her work, in its commitment to disrupting gender and sexual binaries, prefigures the Chicana lesbian feminist concerns of the later twentieth century and beyond.

The conclusion revisits the case of the San Antonio Four, including Deborah Esquenazi's documentary *Southwest of Salem*, to consider its broader implications. I also consider how an unpublished short story by Gloria Anzaldúa may have gestured toward her own understanding of queer gender variance by situating a hybrid female/male character as an interlocutor of the erotics of Chicanx self-making. In addition, I discuss a short story by trans author Claire Jackson, whose work centers the experience of a fictionalized trans woman.

The conclusion's title, "From a Long Line of Marimachas," riffs on Cherríe Moraga's "From a Long Line of Vendidas," a prose piece in her mixed-genre book *Loving in the War Years: Lo Que Nunca Pasó Por Sus Labios*. Moraga describes herself as a Chicana lesbian coming from a long line of traitorous women who have resisted the limiting roles prescribed for them by their families.[19] Moraga says that "[t]he concept of betraying one's race through sex and sexual politics is as common as corn" (103). To her formulation we can add gender variance as a way that Chicanxs challenge the limits of Chicanidad.

The term "marimacha" derives from "marimacho," one of many words used to describe a lesbian. Marimacha can mean "lesbian," or it can mean a masculine woman or butch.[20] As Alicia Arrizón suggests in *Queering Mestizaje*, marimacha can be understood as "a location where gender is fluid and destabilized" (162).[21] According to Richard T. Rodríguez in his book *Next of Kin*, "the use of mach*a* feminizes"[22] terms such as "macho" and "marimacho" and "signif[ies] a variety of contested meanings" (50). It is such contested meanings that I explore in this book.

"Marimacha" also has more expansive possibilities that resonate with genderqueerness and other nonconforming genders. For some, "marimacha" continues to function as a slur. The term also has associations with deviations from "marianismo"; moreover, "macho" functions as a term to identify a male animal (as opposed to "hembra" for a female animal). For many, however, "marimacha" has undergone a reclamation akin to the transformation of the word "queer."[23] Some of the writers, characters, and figures represented here identify as or challenge meanings of "marimacha," while others explore a range of gender variant identities, embodiments, and experiences. As such, "marimacha" is not an umbrella term but rather a locus of exploration that allows us to examine the possibilities for gender variance and gender variant critique in relation to Chicana cultural productions. The genealogy I offer of gender variant subjects and gender variant critiques in Chicana literature situates these texts within a long history of cultural productions by or about marimachas and related figures, expanding the available archive of marimacha, marimachx, and gender variant genealogies.

Post-Borderlandia expands the analytic categories of gender and sexuality to account for racialized queer genders beyond feminine/masculine and homosexual/heterosexual binaries. The book asserts the significance of gender variant critique for examining the relationship between gender and sexuality in Chicana literature and culture. Investigations of these intersecting relationships, especially within Chicanx studies, have not fully taken into account the myriad genders and ways that gender variance reconfigures notions of Chicanidad. Tracking gender variant subjects via figures such as transgender persons, butch Chicanxs, and other gender variant subjects and subjectivities shows how these nonnormative genders inflect how racialized and ethnic subjectivities get constituted. By approaching gender and sexuality as multivalent categories of analysis, *Post-Borderlandia* counters the received notion that Chicana lesbian literature began and peaked in the late twentieth century and situates queerness as a formidable yet unacknowledged presence in the formation of the Chicanax literary canon and cultural imaginaries. Putting forth a paradigm of gender variant critique, I show how post-borderlands Chicana literature works to unsettle the dominant sex/gender binaries by demanding a feminist response that does not always assume "women" as the primary signifier through which to demand gender justice.

Chicana Masculinities

'Lesbian' doesn't name anything in my homeland.
—Gloria Anzaldúa, "To(o) Queer the Writer—
Loca, escritora y chicana"

It is our experience that all language for talking
about butches and fems is inadequate.
—Liz Kennedy and Madeline Davis,
Boots of Leather, Slippers of Gold

I am going back to all those streets to work the
pain. The pain is never going to work me.
—Chonch Fonseca, the butch protagonist
in *The Barber of East L.A.*

Three young butch Latinas in black suits stand on the steps of a spiral staircase. Two of them stare directly at the camera, intent on holding the viewer's gaze. One looks off into the distance, as if noticing someone or something more important beyond the horizon. The butch who stands front and center appears to be the group's jefe, with the other two manly women flanking her, home-bois at her back. The staircase curves upward out of the frame. A message, emblazoned in red and bold uppercase, is superimposed over the black-and-white photograph: "Smart butches exist.

They have opinions. They have feelings. They have politics, too." The message ends with contact information and a call to book the group for public performances, making it clear that this is a promotional flyer. The women are the Butchlalis de Panochtitlan, a performance troupe composed of Mari García, Raquel Gutiérrez, and Claudia Rodríguez. The physical posturing combined with the defensive rhetoric seems designed to simultaneously inspire radical queer identification and incite confusion from the conservatively straight and straitlaced. Apparently the Butchlalis did not get the mainstream memo about the assimilationist gay agenda that encourages queers to make nice and act normal. Or, more accurately, they did get the memo, and this is their creative retort. So, why are these butches ready to throw down? Who are they talking to? And where did they get those fabulous suits?

In their provocative performances, the Butchlalis enact what queer activists Marcia Ochoa and Nancy Mirabal call "*tetatúd*, assembled from the phrase *actitud con tetas* (attitude with tits)," perhaps bound or purposefully hidden in this case, an in-your-face stance toward Latina sexuality (J. Rodríguez 67). The promotional flyer uses the term "tetatúd" to challenge a matched set of cultural assumptions: butches don't think, don't care, don't feel, don't act. These cultural assumptions associate the lack of thinking, caring, feeling, or acting with traditionally restrictive and limiting masculinity. The Butchlalis' message raises critical questions about the cultural work of butchness. What does it mean to think, opine, and feel butch or butchly? What are butch politics? More broadly, what are the contemporary challenges posed to and by the circuits of butch-femme desire and lesbian gender? Cultural productions and interventions such as those by the Butchlalis offer radical possibilities for reworking understandings of butch as racialized sexuality. This chapter looks to such Chicana butch literary and cultural productions to grapple with these questions in illuminating the psychological and cultural geographies of Chicana lesbian borderlands experience.

In Chicana lesbian literature and performance, the figure of the butch is not hard to find. In this chapter, I examine the tendency in Chicana literature to use butchness or masculinity to signify lesbianness, such as in the butch works of Cherríe Moraga and Rocky Gámez. These authors utilize the figures of the strong butch, the failed butch, the baby butch, and the protoqueer tomboy to expose and embrace the sexual and emotional vulnerability of Chicana borderlands butchness. I will focus on the underexamined short fiction of Rocky Gámez, whose work has been anthologized but not often discussed in critical texts. After demonstrating how Gámez's and Moraga's texts helped lay the groundwork for establishing the butch as a prominent Chicana queer figure, I examine how a new generation of Chicana writers and performance artists stage Chicana butchness. I turn to butch performance because, as critic Alicia Arrizón points out in *Latina Performance*, performance "becomes a vehicle through which the body is 'exposed' and multiply delineated" (73), thereby exposing the intersections of queerness through the performance and performativity of gender and sexuality. Through readings of Adelina Anthony's "Mastering Sex and Tortillas" and the Butchlalis de Panochtitlan's *Barber of East L.A.*, I consider how this new order of Chicana butches both draws on and critiques traditional Chicana butchness. Throughout my reading of these texts, I remain attentive to questions of what butch means in a Chicana context. Specifically, I am interested in the Chicana butch struggle to find a place within the Chicanx community, how and why the butch Chicana gets displaced, and the effects of Chicana butch (dis)placements on the constructions of Chicanidad and queerness.

Within a queer Chicanx context, a butch might be described by a variety of culturally specific terms. While the terms "tortillera," "jota," and "lesbiana" might be used to describe a Chicana lesbian, they refer generally to the category of sexuality, to women who sexually desire other women. They do not necessarily specify the gender expression, gender identity, or gender orientation of a Chicana lesbian. A tortillera, jota, or lesbiana might be feminine or masculine, genderqueer, or transgender or might exhibit a widely divergent range of other genders. While the term "lesbiana" has gained increased usage in the past decade, it seems to circulate primarily within academic realms. In "To(o) Queer the Writer," cultural theorist Gloria Anzaldúa rejected the term "lesbian" and the translated "lesbiana" as not resonating with her experience as a queer Tejana, or Mexican Texan: "For me the term lesbian *es problemón*. As a working-class Chicana, mestiza—a composite being, *amalgama de culturas y de lenguas*—a woman who loves women, 'lesbian' is a cerebral word, white and middle-class, representing an English-only dominant culture, derived from the Greek word *lesbos*" (263). For Anzaldúa, being a mestiza/mixed-race person and being an amalgam of cultures and languages required a mixture of terms. Being a Chicana woman who loves women required at the very least a culturally specific term, and Anzaldúa identified "most closely with the Nahuatl term 'patlache,'" which describes a woman who forms an intimate connection with another woman. Patlache, however, is not a gendered or queerly gendered term for "lesbian."

When referring to a masculine Chicana lesbian in particular, some might use the term "chingona," which refers to a badass, one who expresses attitude or cockiness. Chingona distinguishes one from la chingada, or "the fucked one," a vulgar colloquialism for La Malinche, or Malintzín, purportedly the mistress of Hernán Cortés and often cast by Mexican legend as both the mother and the betrayer of the Mexican mestizo people. As a chingona, a Chicana butch is not only one who prefers to fuck rather than be fucked in terms of lesbian sex but is also one who fucks gender, fucks with gender, fucks things up, questions the boundaries and limits of traditional authority. In a queer or lesbian Chicana context, particularly in the S/M subculture, a chingona might also refer to a top, or one who tops, dominates, or controls the sexual scene. Cherríe Moraga asserts that being chingona signifies a desirable position of power: "Nobody wants to be made to feel the turtle with its underside all exposed, just pink and folded flesh. In the effort to avoid embodying la chingada, I became the chingón" (*Loving in the War Years* 125). Whatever the particulars of a Chicana dyke's sexual practices may be, the stance of the chingona offers radical opposition to the mestiza chingada.

Moraga also articulates her chingonaness in *Loving in the War Years* as a desire to move a woman emotionally and physically—literally move a woman, in bed and on the dance floor:

And I move women around the floor, too—women I think
enamored with me. My mother's words rising up from inside
me—'A *real* man, when he dances with you, you'll know he's a
real man by how he holds you in the back.' I think *yes,* someone
who can guide you around a dance floor and so, I do.

Moving these women kindly, surely, even superior. *I can handle
these women.* They want this. And I do too. (31–32)

As Moraga works to untangle her understanding of her own butch
orientation in her mixed-genre memoir, she complicates Chicana
butchness beyond this initial description of a simple desire to control other women's bodies physically.

Chicana literary critic Yvonne Yarbro-Bejarano's astute and in-
depth readings of Moraga's writings offer insight into Moraga's
conception of the relationship between her sexual self and her gendered self. In *The Wounded Heart,* Yarbro-Bejarano says of Moraga's
writing that "[i]n the writing of butch and *chingón* identifications
as both sexual and gender constructions, Moraga's texts undertake
a reading of cultural indoctrination and attempt to come to terms
with it by representing lesbian sex, specifically butch-femme identifications, as one imaginable engagement with the stigmatization
of dominating-dominated polarities" (106). Moraga's exemplifica-
tion of Chicana butch opens up the dominating-dominated binary
even beyond Yarbro-Bejarano's estimation. Chingona as a racialized gendered sexuality is not just about dominating in the style of
the colonizer. For the Chicana butch, it can be about embodying
the capacity to move others sensuously, sexually, and emotionally,
which requires a facility with emotional expressiveness and empa-
thy for the other.

Noting the often misrecognized butch capacity for feeling,
queer theorist Ann Cvetkovich discusses Moraga's butch expression and expressiveness as an emotional style. In the essay titled
"Untouchability and Vulnerability: Stone Butchness as Emotional
Style" published in *Butch/Femme: Inside Lesbian Gender,* Cvetkovich asserts that butch is more than a visual or sexual style. Cvetkovich discusses "butchness as an emotional style, that is, as a set of

conventions for expressing feeling" (159). Cvetkovich explains that in Moraga's butch writing, "[e]specially charged are the connections between penetration, public humiliation, and feminization" (162). According to Cvetkovich, Moraga is able to construct "butch identity in ways that do not demand a rejection of female vulnerability or womanliness, especially a femininity defined in terms of the capacity to feel" (163). It is noteworthy that Moraga negotiates these connections within a specifically Chicanx context. Cvetkovich elaborates by noting how "Moraga's understanding of butch sexuality as a response to colonialism's structures of feeling offers testimony to the difficulty of representing feeling in terms other than stigmatized notions of vulnerability. The value of butch discourse is its power to articulate experiences of feeling that are not castigated as feminine or expected to take forms associated with mental and emotional health, such as openness or expressiveness" (164). Cvetkovich's explanation of butch as emotional style helps us read Moraga's butch emotional style as a chingona. As Moraga's butch persona adopts an outward or visible masculinity, she can also be read as embodying an empowering form of gendered, feminine vulnerability.

Chingona as a Chicana butch gender orientation finds some synergy with Carol Queen's descriptions of working-class butch. In *Real Live Nude Girl*, Queen offers a definition of butch that registers the tension between masculine and feminine and between visual and emotional styles by describing one of her lovers. She says that butch means "so deeply Not Feminine." In the chapter titled "Why I Love Butch Women," Queen says that butch is walking down the street with attitude, wearing jeans and white T-shirts, and exhibiting "the kind of womanness that isn't taught in school," marking butch as nonconformist, nonacademic, and circulating in a working-class street culture. Queen goes on to say that "[b]utch is a giant *Fuck YOU!* to compulsory femininity, just as lesbianism says the same to compulsory heterosexuality" (153). Emphasizing how butch, like femme, crosses traditional gender boundaries, Queen declares that "I love butch women because, in their big black boots, they step squarely across a line" (160). This juxtaposition of the not-feminine physical style and attitude with what Cvetkovich describes as a feminine emotional style makes it difficult to ascertain the gender of butch. In *Butch Is a Noun*, S. Bear Bergman professes to "know what butch is" and offers a humorous definition that contradicts itself every step of the way.[1] For Chicana and other racialized butches, butch may be a matter of mixing sexual style with visual style as well as emotional style. The concept of butch itself is inherently contradictory—and in the cultural work this chapter explores, Chicana butch mixes genders to construct a borderlands gender that resonates with the notion of mestizaje.[2] This borderlands gender is a way of feeling butch along the lines of Muñoz's "Feeling Brown," an "affective overload" born of exceeding normative categories of Latinidad.

Butch as a category of lesbian gender continues to be subject(ed) to definitional debates, suggesting its resistance to fixedness. Debates around butchness also signal ongoing attempts to regulate gender as well as unseat it from its regulatory throne. The visible butch often gets read by the dominant gaze as a mode of cultural loss, wherein expressions of masculinity may be perceived merely as failed femininity. This misreading sets up the butch figure as inherently antifeminine, conceptually trapping the definition of butch as against woman—and as a lesbian she is often assumed to be antiman. So, if the butch is only allowed to be considered man-hating and woman-hating, what is she presumed to be and to be for? Can butch identity be fully explained in terms of what Muñoz terms "disidentification," the disavowal of the normative or dominative, and if so to what effect?

According to Judith Butler, butch and femme are "historical identities of sexual style" (*Gender Trouble* 41). For Butler, butch identity involves the juxtaposition of masculine and feminine, particularly through the resignification of the masculine:

> Within lesbian contexts, the "identification" with masculinity that appears as butch identity is not a simple assimilation of lesbianism back into the terms of heterosexuality. As one lesbian femme explained, she likes her boys to be girls, meaning that "being a girl"

contextualizes and resignifies "masculinity" in a butch identity. As a result, that masculinity, if that it can be called, is always brought into relief against a culturally intelligible "female body." (156)

In Butler's formulation, butch requires the presence of a readable "female body" onto which traditionally masculine codes can be reconstituted as a lesbian gender expression. The butch's subversive appropriation of masculinity for expression and use in what Butler refers to as "lesbian contexts" troubles the gender binary not just by mixing genders but also by intersecting gender expression with transgressive sexual orientation.

Representations of Chicana butchness explore a range of aspects of queer, masculine, working-class Chicana experience. In doing so, Chicana butch texts shift dominant discourses about butchness. One dominant misconception is the trite idea that butch is a retrograde or misogynist form of gender identity or expression. The second is the idea that butch fell out of favor and then reemerged onto the lesbian public scene. Addressing the first idea, Jack Halberstam's work in theorizing "female masculinity" attempts to recuperate butch and other masculine lesbian genders by recognizing them as existing along complex continua of queer genders and sexualities. But the texts I will examine in this chapter also stretch the boundaries of gender expression to account for valences of race/ethnicity and class, and they engage masculinity, and butch masculinity in particular, as much more than a consciously adopted performance or matter of style.

The Chicana lesbian and queer cultural productions I examine in this chapter resist both of these dominant, limiting tropes of butchness. They also construct a particular idea of butch by interrogating how butch is racialized and gendered specifically in a Chicanx context. Within a Chicanx context, the butch figures in the texts I discuss here connect their sense of being butch with obtaining class mobility and cultural capital among other Chicanxs.

Many other writers and scholars have taken up discussions of butch lesbian gender, with many focusing on its matter of visual style and its tenuous and shifting relationship to feminisms, including lesbian feminisms (Nestle; Kennedy and Davis; Faderman; Burana and Due; Halberstam; Munt). These valuable contributions to queer thought have helped document and legitimize butch and butch-femme as lesbian identity formations. Yet, few considerations of butch-femme in mainstream queer academic discourse adequately consider the relation between race or ethnicity to sexuality and gender. For my purposes, I am interested in how Chicana authors represent butch within Chicano and Chicanx contexts, complicating the interconnectedness of identity formations along the lines of race, ethnicity, class, sexuality, sex, gender, and gender expression.

The short fiction of Rocky Gámez, a writer from the lower Rio Grande Valley of South Texas, provides a lens into the Chicana butch struggle to find a sense of belonging within Chicano community. Gámez's series of short stories centers around a working-class Tejana butch named Gloria, whose adventures are narrated by the character of Rocky. Gloria is a working-class lesbiana who lives in the Rio Grande Valley of South Texas, and her friend Rocky is a lesbiana from the valley who has moved away to go to college. The first of the stories, called "From *The Gloria Stories*," was originally published in the journal *Conditions* in 1981 and has been anthologized in collections such as *Cuentos: Stories by Latinas* (1983), edited by Moraga et al., and Joan Nestle's iconic project *The Persistent Desire: A Femme-Butch Reader* (1992). The other two Gloria stories include "A Baby for Adela" and "A Matter of Fact," and all three deal with Gloria's desire to impregnate her girlfriend.

"From *The Gloria Stories*" begins with Rocky reminiscing about the "ridiculous" childhood aspirations she had: "I remember wanting to be an acolyte so badly I would go around bobbing in front of every icon I came across whether they were in churches or private houses. When this aspiration was forgotten, I wanted to be a kamikaze pilot so I could nosedive into the church that never allowed girls to serve at the altar" (202). The first image characterizes the young Rocky as an adoringly attentive, devoted altar boy who is eager to please, while the second imagines a type of violent fantasy typically associated with traditional boys' play as a means for actively resisting institutionalized gender inequity in the Catholic Church.

Then, Rocky claims to have changed as she grew up: "After that I made a big transition. I wanted to be a nurse, then a doctor, then a burlesque dancer, and finally I chose to be a schoolteacher. Everything else was soon forgiven and forgotten" (202). Notably, she goes from wishing for a traditionally feminine occupation to a traditionally masculine one to a blatantly pro–sex entertainment career and back to a traditionally feminine, normative mainstream occupation: schoolteacher. Rocky's aspirations are then contrasted with Gloria's: "My friend Gloria, however, never went beyond aspiring to be one thing, and one thing only. She wanted to be a man" (202).

Rocky writes home to Gloria because she has heard rumors from friends in her hometown that Gloria has been going around dressed in drag, drinking heavily, and consorting with prostitutes. Rocky is alarmed at the news from her sister about Gloria:

> One letter said that she [Rocky's sister] has spotted her in the darkness of a theater making out with another girl. Another letter said that she had seen Gloria coming out of a cantina with her arms hooked around two whores. But the most disturbing one was when she said that she had seen Gloria at a 7–11 convenience store, with a butch haircut and what appeared to be dark powder on the sides of her face to imitate a beard. (202)

Of concern to Rocky is her friend Gloria's public displays of gender and sexual nonconformity in a region bound by the strong traditions of a conservative and predominantly Catholic working-class Mexican and Mexican American population. Also of concern to Rocky is Gloria's obsession with reproduction and her claim that she has the ability to get her girlfriend pregnant.

Rocky, whose own name strikes a Chicana butch chord, as "Rocky" or "Raque" can be a nickname for the name Raquel, seems oddly confused not by Gloria's sexual orientation or objects of desire but rather by her gender expression as overly mannish or masculine. Rocky responds by writing a letter to Gloria: "I quickly sat down and wrote her a letter expressing my concern and questioning her sanity." Gloria writes back to the friend, admitting to the behaviors and recounting the story of how she recently asked her girlfriend to marry her. The epistolary form details the exchange between the two friends across distance and gives way to prose narration when injuries from a car accident send Rocky back to the Rio Grande Valley to recuperate.

Besides the distance of geography, there is the distance between the educational attainment of the two friends, as Rocky had left home to go to college while Gloria remained in the valley to work. In another story in the Gloria series, Gloria quits her slaughterhouse job so that she and Rocky can work together selling brooms door-to-door. Because Rocky left for college away from the Rio Grande Valley, which has two universities that serve a predominantly Mexican American student population, we can perhaps presume that Rocky attends a faraway college at a predominantly white institution. Rocky, when she comes home to intervene in Gloria's life, can be read as the voice of urban, educated, white feminists who engaged in dismissing butchness as undesirable or at the very least outmoded. This dismissal of butch and butch-femme gendered sexuality as a possible expression for lesbians can be found in works such as Del Martin and Phyllis Lyon's *Lesbian/Woman*, in which Martin and Lyon charge that "[t]he minority of Lesbians who still cling to the traditional male-female or husband-wife pattern in their partnerships are more than likely old-timers, gay bar habituées, or working class women" (77). To their wholesale category of working-class women, one could add women of color as practitioners of butch-femme expression or identity. Gámez critiques this line of thinking that attempts to discount the legitimacy or continued presence of butches and femmes in queer communities.

Like Gámez, Adelina Anthony's theatrical work raises questions about the significant cultural work of butch gender in queer Chicana communities. Her solo performance *Mastering Sex and Tortillas* has toured around the United States, mostly in queer community centers and on college campuses (Figure 3). *Mastering*

FIGURE 3. Adelina Anthony as Papi Duro and Mama Chocha in her solo performance *Mastering Sex and Tortillas.* Photo by Weenobee.

Sex and Tortillas stages the Chicana femme and the Chicana butch as inextricably connected yet often at odds—with themselves, with each other, with other queers, and with other Chicanxs.

Originally from San Antonio and now based in Los Angeles, Anthony is the founding director of a Los Angeles–based community organization called Lives United through Community, History, and Art and is a film producer and the director of AdeRisa Productions as well as the director of a performance group called Teatro Q, which develops community-based theater in collaboration with other queer Latinx performers. Anthony's career was bolstered by her collaboration with Cherríe Moraga. Anthony directed Moraga's *Hungry Woman: A Mexican Medea* at a community theater in Dallas before going to Stanford to study with Moraga in the graduate theater program, which Anthony left after a year to work as a full-time artist, citing what she describes as ideological differences between her aesthetics and politics and the program's traditional approach.[3]

Anthony chooses to identify herself as a "Xiqana," which has implications for how she shapes her performances around intersecting themes of race and sexuality. Like many other self-proclaimed Xicana feministas, Anthony uses the "X" as a reclamation of the Nahautl pronunciation of the letter "X" with a "ch" or "sh" sound and a rejection of the Spanish colonizers' mistranslation of Nahuatl words. According to Anthony, she also changes the middle letter in the traditional "Chicana" from a "c" to a "q" to signify queerness. Anthony describes her queerness as bound together with her Mexican and indigenous identities. Her decolonial politic seeks to rework language in order to accommodate her experience as a Xiqana.

The first time I saw Adelina Anthony do her solo performance *Mastering Sex and Tortillas* was in East Austin at the Historic Victory Grill, a treasured gathering place for working-class black folks, musicians, poets, activists, and queers of color. It is the kind of place that has shower curtains separating the two toilets in the women's bathroom into makeshift stalls. To get to the back stall, you have to open the curtains and step through the first stall into the second, making this an awkward social maneuver when the first stall is occupied. And when you go to the bar, you better have cash—preferably small bills because they might not have much change on hand. And whatever you do, do not ask for a fancy hipster drink or trendy imported beer. In other words, it is the kind of place where folks like me feel right at home, having grown up in a small barrio with at least four neighborhood cantinas, one of which operated out of a couple's silver mobile home trailer in a parking lot. The bar next door, called the Playroom, the one most frequented by my family, extended family, and neighbors, had two nice bartenders, a middle-aged Mexicana and a young Mexicano who called me by name, gave me free drinks, and never minded when I played the same song on the juke box over and over while I played pool. I was seven years old. The drinks were merely sodas, and I was often to be found sitting in a booth doing my homework while my family hung out on weekend and some weekday evenings. Perhaps my fond memories of the Playroom make the Victory Grill feel like arriving home. Or perhaps it is that the first year I lived in Austin I had the good fortune to read poetry on stage there, alongside Joe Jimenez, Corrie Sublett-Berrios, and Pedro Pietri.

The night Adelina Anthony performed, the house was packed mostly with local queer activists and writers as well as academics in town to attend the conference of the National Association of Chicana and Chicano Studies. I had met Adelina but had yet to see her perform in person. Fifteen minutes after the show was scheduled to begin, people were still milling about when a woman stormed into the performance space from the grill area through the bar area. She was yelling something, and people were moving to get out of her way. Given my childhood barroom training, I assumed that it was somebody who had tried to save a buck by getting drunk at home before coming to the bar and now she was pissed because they would not serve her any more alcohol. But when the spotlight lit up her face, I realized that it must be the performer making a dramatic entrance, wearing dark sunglasses, crashing through the door, and yelling like a loca. The woman was wearing a very tight, very short black skirt that barely covered her nalgas, and she was tugging at the bottom of the skirt to keep it down while she walked through the crowd. Her curly hair was pinned up on the back of her head, with curls escaping here and there. And she was holding a cell phone to her ear, saying "Ay,

Dolores, mi amor, mi vida, of course I love you." The performance had indeed begun.

The performer proceeds onto the stage, continuing with the intimate phone call being broadcast via wireless microphone. When she arrives at center stage, she sets her large purse on the table—the only object on stage—and turns to face the audience. She squeals with delight at the sight of the audience and puts the phone down to speak directly to the crowd. She announces that she is "La Profesora Mama Chocha" and welcomes us to her "seminar on how to become a tortillera" (lesbian or dyke).

For the first half of the performance Mama Chocha leads the tortillera seminar, bantering with the audience and claiming that she will teach them how to become "true tortilleras." After intermission, the solo performer arrives on stage as a new character. Similar to the previous dramatic entrance, this character bursts forth into the audience from a side door. This time, however, she is dressed in khakis, a work shirt, and a fedora, symbols of working-class Chicana butchness. She wields a three-foot-long dildo like a gun and announces herself as "Papi Duro, F.B.I." While she doesn't explain that her name translates as "Hard Daddy," she does spell out that "F.B.I." stands for "Fearless Bucha Instigator." Over the course of this second act, the character is revealed to be an "old-school butch" who reminisces about the movimiento days and wants to pass on her knowledge to young "baby buchas" (butches) in the audience.

In a critical scene that questions the misogynistic tendencies associated with "old-school" or traditionally masculinist forms of butch behavior toward other women, Papi Duro struggles with being faithful to her femme lover. Papi Duro interacts with audience members and at one point accuses a butch in the audience of having an affair with Papi Duro's femme girlfriend, playing into the idea that Latina butches are oversexed players but also breaking down the paradox of the old-school butch paradigm. Anthony starts to critique the sexual double standard by way of this public "confrontation" with the audience. After she receives a package from her girlfriend challenging Papi Duro on her own affair and threatening to break up, she realizes that her girlfriend is no longer willing to put up with the double standard of the loyal femme and philandering man/butch/macho/a as a sustainable paradigm of masculinity. It is in that moment that the performance questions the viability of a butch identity that hinges on a kind of sexual prowess that disrespects femmes or disregards the traditionally closed circuit of a monogamous butch-femme ethic. Papi has expressed consciousness as a butch and as a Chicana activist and in this moment experiences a coming to consciousness around feminist and woman-to-woman solidarity.

In another critical scene, Papi Duro poses as a Mexican gardener to solicit money from rich "gringa" Beverly Hills housewives. In a structure similar to that of the first act, modeled after an instructional seminar, the character provides the audience with tips on how a butch lesbiana can pose as a Mexican gardener in order to seduce rich housewives for money. In this scene, Anthony critiques multiple mainstream U.S. cultural assumptions about Latinxs. Papi Duro expressly plays into the Latin lover stereotype in order to "raise funds for la causa":

> So, if you get selected for Operation Gaykeeper your role is not only to follow in my Papi Duro footsteps & be like a Mexican jumping bean, hopping from one bed to another leaving mujeres with a sense of their own poder, or at least with a sense of multiple orgasms. But in addition, as a 21st century F.B.I. agent you'll be asked to do the most dreadful, taxing, mind-boggling work of any grassroots movement. Oh, yes, people, I'm asking you to fund-raise!

Merging the idea of the special agent or government operative with the idea of the activist as an agent of social change, the butches chosen by Papi Duro to join her as Fearless Butch Instigators become responsible for facilitating women's self-empowerment by creating access to sexual pleasure and by raising the economic capital required to support a grassroots movement, presumably for racial, gender, and economic justice. Calling the plan "Operation

Gaykeeper" invokes the perennially relevant history of the U.S. government's "gatekeeping" border operations. Such operations have included the rounding up and deportation of Mexicans, including Mexican Americans born in the United States, as part of the shamelessly named "Operation Wetback" implemented by the U.S. Immigration and Naturalization Service in 1954.

Referring to the effort as an "operation" also pokes fun at the myth of lesbians and gays actively seeking to "recruit" or "convert" unwitting heterosexuals into a "homosexual lifestyle." Rather than recruit straight folks to lesbian life, Papi Duro proclaims the goal of "keeping the women gay" so that they do not feel pressured to succumb to compulsory heterosexuality. This inverts the mainstream fear that lesbians threaten heterosexuals by recruiting women and instead suggests the perhaps equally threatening notion that lesbians threaten compulsory heterosexuality by maintaining satisfaction among lesbians so they will "stay gay." The scene also calls attention to how Latino males who appear to be manual laborers or poor or working class because of their signature dress in khakis and work shirts are often criminalized by systemic racial profiling. Ironically, the character of Papi Duro is indeed engaging in illicit activities by seeking to extort additional money from the wealthy landowning white women of Beverly Hills whose lawns she maintains.

As Papi Duro continues the "butch training" lesson for the audience, she outlines the requirements for the job. As transgressors across multiple borders, Papi Duro explains, the butch instigators will have to be discreet as well as resourceful: "But, there's a catch, esas, in order to avoid detection in your social, sexual, and geographical border crossings you're being asked to go under the covers without your modern-day tools." As she says this, she pulls several dildos and a set of handcuffs out of her baggy pants pockets and throws them aside. Continuing with the lesson for the young butches, Papi Duro proceeds to describe the kinds of tools they will be allowed to use. She drags a briefcase onto the stage and starts pulling objects out of it. From the suitcase, she reveals a pair of wooden-handled hedge clippers and holds them up to the audience, declaring that the butch agent can use the shears as fingernail clippers, suggesting that short fingernails are a visible sign of butch identity or are requisite for butch sexual prowess. She then asks the audience what they will do if they do not have access to sex toys:

> And think about it—a real migrant worker can't be affording no $50 dildos. So, special agents, basically, if I say to you "No dildos!" then you say "No problemo, Papi Duro, you said I'm a Beverly Hills jardinero, pos aquí tengo mi pepino." [She then pulls out a cucumber.] Chingao, it's even organic!

As she pulls out the third and final item from the briefcase, Papi Duro declares triumphantly "No store-bought lubricants? I got my all-purpose savila!" The item she holds up for display is a large aloe vera leaf, a traditional folk healing plant among Mexican Americans. "Personally," she goes on to say, "I swear by my abuelita's aloe vera." Papi Duro puts these common objects into service as the butch lesbian's "tools." She takes the accoutrements associated with the gardener for hire, in this case "the Mexican gardener," and reassigns them as accessories associated with lesbian sex. By resignifying these common objects, "Mastering Sex and Tortillas" enacts a queer version of what theorist and artist Amalia Mesa-Bains calls rasquache domesticana. According to Mesa-Bains, Chicanas in art and in everyday life have transformed domestic objects into artful expressions in order to fulfill basic needs. The rasquache domesticana is the feminine counterpart to Chicano rasquache, which refers to the resourceful art of making something from nearly nothing or using a common object for a creative or unexpected purpose, such as using gardening shears to trim one's fingernails in the absence of fingernail clippers.

Anthony queers the rasquache by making use of workers' tools for women to engage in sex with other women.[4] By noting that Chicana lesbianas have resorted to various tactics of survival in order to find each other and engage in sexual liaisons, Anthony deploys the cultural concept of rasquachismo for the express purpose of making lesbian and queer desire and pleasure possible. Thus, Anthony mobilizes an erotics of power, playing with the stigmas attached to Mexican gardeners as well as to cross-racial same-sex desire. In this way, Anthony appeals to the audience's sympathy by claiming to be working for a noble cause, la causa, that of racial equity and social justice for Mexicans, Mexican Americans, and Latinxs.

Through the themes of fidelity to butch-femme structures of desire and the role of lesbianas in the civil rights movements, Anthony emphasizes the pivotal place of Chicana butches in developing queer communities within and across racial bounds. Her nuanced critique and reworking of Chicana butchness places a value on butch expression within Chicana lesbian or queer contexts and positions the butch as a potentially powerful and threatening figure to a racist, heterosexist status quo. As a "role model" for the aspiring butches in the audience, the character of Papi Duro also becomes a community mentor intent on imparting sexual knowledge. As such, Anthony performs a sex-positive, risque, unapologetically irreverent approach to passing on Chicana lesbiana cultural knowledge. Her performance pays tribute to old-school Chicana butches who were involved in the Chicano movement and also asserts that the contemporary Chicana butch must consciously choose which aspects of traditional Chicana butch identity to sustain and which to shed. Anthony effectively embodies the place of butch in the larger Chicanx movement, with Papi Duro arguing for a movement of Chicana butch identity beyond the historical or nostalgic.

Adelina Anthony takes another foray into creating butch and other gender-nonconforming characters who tackle even heavier topics in her feature film *Bruising for Besos*. The film centers the experiences of a queer Chicana struggling with questions of violence in her family of origin, in her dating relationships, and in her present-day chosen queer familia. Emerging as a theater project, *Bruising for Besos* has evolved into a full-length feature film released in 2017 by AdeRisa Productions, a production company that Anthony runs with her spouse Marisa Becerra.

The filmmaker's website describes the protagonist of *Bruising for Besos*, Yoli Villamontes, as "a charismatic Xicana lesbian making familia in a queer/trans people of color scene in Los Angeles." Dino Foxx notes that the character of Yoli "is named for the Nahuatl derivative of 'yolotl,' which means 'heart'" (n.p.). The film follows Yoli, who lives with her best friend Rani, as she develops a new relationship with Daña. Through various dramatic encounters, Yoli begins to detect disturbing patterns of behavior from Daña. As glimpses into Yoli's childhood reveal a history of family violence, Yoli grows determined not to repeat the harmful patterns. Gender variance becomes a matter of contention at various points in the film, as various characters express confusion about a transgender character. Additionally, Yoli contends with the entanglement of hegemonic masculinity and violence as enacted by people with various kinds of bodies and identities, emphasizing how violence can be perpetrated by anyone. A crucial plot line revolves around how Yoli responds to the knowledge that violence can be used a tool of domination not merely by men in her family but also by high femme love interests (Figure 4).

In facing how violence has affected her family of origin and continues to haunt her current life, Yoli must also come to grips

FIGURE 4. Still image from the film *Bruising for Besos*, written by Adelina Anthony. Produced by Adelina Anthony and Marisa Becerra of AdeRisa Productions.

with her own potential for enacting violence against others. As the various storylines come crashing against each other, she has vivid memories of witnessing violence as a child. As Yoli dreams of her childhood, flashbacks occur within the realm of a puppet world she has created for a project. She makes the puppets by hand, and they resemble papier-mâché marionettes one might purchase from a street vendor in Mexico. The elaborately and brilliantly constructed puppets were made by Love & Monsters Puppet Company of Austin. AdeRisa Productions collaborated with the puppet troupe and commissioned specially designed puppets and miniature sets that have an exquisite rasquacheness to them.

In highly dramatic and pointed scenes, the young Yoli puppet tries to understand and respond to her father's violence toward her mother. For Yoli, going home to see her ill mother becomes a major theme, as her desire to go home is complicated not only by the history of violence in her family of origin but also by the troubles in her new relationships and by her lack of funds to travel home.[5] After obtaining funds from her best friend, Yoli grows ready to return home only when she begins to come to terms with ending the violence in her current relationships. That Yoli's queer butch self desires to remain committed to nonviolence in her relationships speaks to Anthony's creative desire to have the film construct a narrative of healing (Anthony, "Introduction: Bruising for Besos" 62). Anthony's characteristic humor, coupled with an engaging take on Yoli's struggles with facing violence, makes a strong contribution as a queer Chicana feature film that centers gender variance as an important vector in the story.

Like Adelina Anthony and Rocky Gámez, the Butchlalis of Panochtitlan construct complex renderings of the Chicana butch. The Butchlalis of Panochtitlan are a performance troupe consisting of three core members: Raquel Gutiérrez, Mari García, and Claudia Rodríguez. Some of their shows have included a fourth member or guest performer. The group's name riffs on Tenochtitlan, now Mexico City, built on the ancient Mexica capital and the site of the promised land of the Mexica upon their departure from the legendary homeland of Aztlán. Chicanoizing the sacred city's name, the Butchlalis replace the first part of the word "tenochca" (another term for Mexica or Aztec peoples) with "panocha," considered vulgar Mexican/Chicano slang for "vagina." Thus, the Butchlalis declare themselves to be of the holy capital of pussylandia.

In *The Barber of East L.A.*, the Butchlalis locate themselves not only in the imagined sacred land of Panochtitlan but also in the city of Los Angeles, particularly in East L.A., in its ongoing struggles against gentrification (Figure 5). A staged production of *The Barber of East L.A.* played in 2009 at the Jump-Start Performance Company in San Antonio and was directed by Luis Alfaro, known for his queer solo performance. It was a sold-out show, with a large contingent from allgo's Austin-based queer community joining the San Antonio crowd. The spare stage was set with a long table lined with mannequin heads wearing wigs of various styles and colors.

When the lights go up on stage, standing front and center are three Latina butches wearing crisp white guayaberas, blue jeans, and black dress shoes. The bucha in the center has a hairstyle

FIGURE 5. Butchlalis promotional image for their show *The Barber of East L.A.* Image by Hector Silva.

cresting in front to suggest a slight pompadour. The troupe opens the first act like a doo-wop vocal group, dressed alike and moving in unison. Together they chant their opening rhyme:

There's a butch in every barrio
There's a butch in every 'hood
Every barrio has its macha
Not every barrio treats her good (Gutiérrez, "The Barber of
    East L.A.")

The terms "barrio" and "'hood" establish a place that looms somewhere between the specific (given the naming of East L.A. in the play's title) and the universal, as the signifier "barrio" can refer to any neighborhood with a significant Latinx presence.

The use of "butch" and "macha" signal not just a Chicanx or Latinx framework but also a working-class one, as "macha" tends to be used as a slang term, derived from "marimacho" or "marimacha." The first three lines claim the butch's ubiquitous presence across barrios, while the final line suggests that the macha/butch may be subject to mistreatment or harassment and locates her as an Other within a Chicanx/Latinx neighborhood community. While typically the neighborhood or barrio serves as the place where Chicanxs make sense to themselves and each other away from a hostile or indifferent dominant culture, the bucha does not always receive such understanding.

Chonch Fonseca, the central protagonist, is described in the script as being "35, Butch Dyke, Latina" (Gutiérrez, "The Barber of East L.A."). In a crucial scene, Chonch explains how she was named by an older Chicana/Latina butch in her neighborhood. Chonch recalls being a young kid looking out the window of a multistory apartment building onto the street and being mesmerized by the sight of an older butch woman and the confident way she stood on the street corner with her girlfriend. She identifies the confusing contradictions of gender expressions embodied by the elder butch, known in the barrio as a woman called Juana Chingas:

I looked out the window and I see . . . her.

Ella. La mas firme de todas.

A bulldagger leaning against the bus stop, doing it like she does
   it every day.

Sabia.

That's where I wanted to live, in her body.

Her broad shoulders fill out the bright blue Pendleton—it makes
   her look like a prince—she wears her pantalones caquis with
   a killer crease.

But it's her HAIR, that does me in! Es puro cholo pompadour!

Elvis, Ritchie Valens and Buddy Holly with hips, tits, lips and
   power. (Gutiérrez, "The Barber of East L.A.")

When the two women on the street corner begin to kiss each other, the young girl watching the scene from the window above the street is so awestruck by what she sees that she blurts out a nonsensical sound: "Choooonch." The older butch Latina on the street looks up to see who is yelling out the window. When the older butch sees the young masculine-looking girl in the window, she calls her by the sound she yelled: "Chonch." The young protagonist says that "[w]hen Juana Chingas hears that come out of my mouth, she laughs real cool and tosses her head back to see who the fuck this traviesa is." Juana Chingas responds with a colloquial greeting akin to "What's up, Chonch?" by saying "Quihubole, Chonch?" Proudly, Chonch recalls of that moment, "She gave me my name" (Gutiérrez, "The Barber of East L.A.").

By saying "She gave me my name," Chonch recognizes the significance of the queer rite of passage she has experienced. In witnessing the desire expressed between two Latina lovers, one butch and one femme, Chonch has no language to describe the specific form of desire she sees, but she knows that it surprises and moves her. The sound she utters becomes an exchange between her and the older butch woman she wants to be like, and together they construct a queer language that names the young butch and the confusing intensity of her gendered desire.

Chonch grows up to become fascinated with butch hairstyles and decides to become a butch barber. As part of her commitment to serving not just her queer community but also the working-class Chicanxs and Latinxs of her East L.A. barrio, Chonch opens her own barbershop after graduating from beauty school. As she struggles to build a modest small business, she also struggles with whether to serve as a role model for the neighborhood's queer kids. On the one hand, Chonch seeks to queer her barrio by being a highly visible butch barber who offers traditionally masculine hair-cuts for women. On the other hand, she worries that her traditional notion of Chicana butch will not provide the younger butches with adequate queer knowledge to survive in a homophobic world, especially in the rough barrio where she must negotiate her complex relationship between her Chicanidad and her queerness.

Arlene Stein, in *Shameless: Sexual Dissidence in American Culture*, claims that "[l]ike ethnic communities, lesbian/gay boundaries, identities, and cultures are negotiated, defined, and produced" (14). Rather than viewing the cultural formations of ethnic communities and lesbian/gay communities as parallel, the queer Chicana cultural and artistic producers in this chapter inspire a revision of Stein's statement to read something like the following: In ethnic communities, lesbian/gay boundaries, identities, and cultures are negotiated, defined, and produced with relation to race and class, and in the process, they contribute to reshaping those communities.

The boundaries and definitions of Chicana butch in the representations I examine in this chapter are indeed culturally distinct from other cultural productions of dominative white butch masculinity. In *The Drag King Book* in the chapter "Class, Race, and Masculinity: The Superfly, the Macdaddy, and the Rapper," Jack Halberstam and Del Lagrace Volcano acknowledge the pervasiveness and ranges of butch-femme visible in women of color communities:

> Interestingly, in predominantly women-of-color queer spaces, in New York at least, many of the women participate in elabo-rate and creative versions of butch-femme style, while the more

white spaces favor a kind of androgynous or alternative aesthetic (piercings and tattoos). Many of the Drag Kings we interviewed in New York attested to a kind of racialized separation of spheres. Since butch-femme already exists within some of the women-of-color spaces as a noticeable style, one might expect that these clubs would produce more Drag King culture. This was not true. (142)

Halberstam and Volcano's attempt to find a connection between butch-femme and drag king culture in women of color queer spaces illustrates the need to disarticulate drag king as a public performative aesthetic style from butch-femme as an always already available gender orientation for queer women of color. Their observation that "butch-femme already exists" for women of color aligns with my assertion that butch-femme among Chicanas, especially working-class Chicanas, did not necessarily experience the same disappearance or backlash as it did among white lesbians in urban centers. Also, the butch-femme "style" that Halberstam and Volcano note in women of color queer communities differs substantively from the public performance of "female masculinity" in drag kinging.

Thinking of Chicana butch as a gender orientation—that is, not just as a gender and/or sexuality identity, which suggests a fixedness, or as gender expression, which can be misread as being too fluid—can provide a productive contextualization of Chicana butch. Sara Ahmed, in *Queer Phenomenology: Orientations, Objects, Others*, echoing Judith Butler, suggests that butch and femme tend to be misread as false copies that mimic heterosexuality because one must also consider the orientation of individuals to their objects of desire. I think that Ahmed's use of "orientation" helps us make sense of how Chicana butches orient themselves not just in terms of their sexual objects of desire but also in terms of their racial/ethnic filiations and affiliations.[6] I contend that the cultural representations of Chicana butchness discussed in this chapter call for an understanding of Chicana butch as not just about a fixed identity or a fluidity of expression but also about a particular gender orientation as it intersects with sexual orientation.

Through my readings of Gámez's, Anthony's, and the Butch-lalis' cultural productions, I offer a reorienting of Chicana butch as a racialized gender orientation, and certainly much more than a fixed identity or adopted style. Adelina Anthony's work serves as an "orientation" for baby butches. Her characters orient new butch agents on how to be butch. Anthony is also performing the cultural work of political orientation, providing young Chicanas with a history of the Chicano movement and the significant role that Chicana lesbian feminists played in organizing for the movement. Anthony's butch orientation calls for an understanding that Chicana butches have a history of serving Chicanx community. Gámez's work is oriented to place, in this case South Texas, and to making sense of how the Chicana butch struggles to find a place for herself within Chicanx community. The butch in *The Barber of East L.A.* is also very oriented to place. For her, East L.A. provides a sense of specific place or home that is threatened by gentrification and by its own potentially self-destructive responses to queerness.

In Carol Queen's account of how she came into her femme identity, she recalls the 1970s as devoid of butch-femme culture: "In the seventies, when I came out into the dyke community, butch was dead and androgyny was practically an imperative" (153). She further characterizes the 1970s as "that decade of butchness diluted and femme reviled" (155). In a 1992 article in the *Journal of the History of Sexuality*, Lillian Faderman chimes in on this popular refrain that butch-femme had fallen away and then reemerged. Faderman's article, "The Return of Butch and Femme: A Phenomenon in Lesbian Sexuality of the 1980s and 1990s," claims that the figure of the butch reappeared in lesbian life and public discourse after an absence of some years, and Faderman uses the term "neo-butch" to capture this apparent resurgence. Faderman's and Queen's accounts, like Nestle's and Stein's, echo the dominant narrative of white middle-class lesbian history in the late twentieth century. The texts I discuss in this chapter suggest that for Chicanas and queer working-class communities of color, the same kind of chronologies or paradigms of lesbian gender and butch-femme cannot be assumed.

While being butch and/or femme may have indeed fallen in and out of favor in some circles for varying reasons of sexual politics, many Chicana lesbian literary and cultural productions indicate an alternative history of what butch-femme means and can mean. When we look to Chicana cultural productions, a narrative of butch-femme beyond Faderman's or Halberstam and Volcano's version comes into view. For Chicanas, butch-femme is not a nueva onda, nor is it a trendy (or passe) movida; instead, it has been a sustained way of being lesbian or queer within a predominantly working-class Chicanx context. The notion that butch-femme ever left the building in the first place is a white lesbian narrative that can exclude as well as unconsciously dismiss how butch-femme may be at work in various working-class and poor queer communities of color, particularly in places distanced from the urban and suburban epicenters of lesbian academic conversations.

Faderman attributes what she calls "neo-butch" to a reaction against 1970s lesbian feminism and also a sense of adventure, both of which assume a monolithic middle-class lesbian frame:

> Although a few women who identified as butch or femme in the 1980s (or at present) [1992] did so with the same deadly seriousness that characterized the women of the 1950s, many others did it out of a sense of adventure, a historical curiosity, a longing to push at the limits. For them neo-butch/femme roles and relationships often maintain the lessons of feminism that lesbians learned from the 1970s. They are more subtle, complex, flexible. There are few contemporary butches who would entertain the notion that they are men trapped in women's bodies. For these reasons, the meaning of butch and femme over the past decade was very different from what it had been thirty or forty years earlier. (579)

There is, to be sure, a certain social mobility and public expression of gender identity and public debate around lesbian and queer assumed in Faderman's argument. The "seriousness" that Faderman acknowledges, yet seems to dismiss, fails to recognize the working-class butch-femme history where daily survival may have been and continued to be rather serious business. Faderman's account of butch-femme misses the mark for the Chicana butch texts, in which Chicana femmes and butches, even in humorous moments, are taken rather seriously. I hope my own textual analyses demonstrate that we cannot simply use dominative frames such as Faderman's piece as a lens to read texts such as the working-class Chicana butch literature of Rocky Gámez. It would be too easy to assume Gámez's piece as an example, proof of Faderman's argument, that there was a resurgence toward butch-femme in the 1980s and 1990s.

The story of lesbian gender becomes a dominant narrative that goes from butch-femme to androgyny to reclaiming butch-femme, a neobutch era. But if we resist imposing this white lesbian paradigm onto queer brown experience and instead allow queer brown texts and lives to theorize themselves, then we see that butchness for some Chicana lesbians is not about riding a stylistic, aesthetic, or political trend. So, when contemporary conversations turn to talk about "butch flight" or when people ask where all the butches have gone, perhaps they need look no further than Rocky Gámez's Rio Grande Valley, the Butchlalis' "East Los," or any working-class barrio where, undoubtedly, buchas, chingonas, and marimachas continue to carve out queer spaces for loving and living as butch Chicanas.

2

Ambiguous Chicanx Bodies

The brown body's ambiguity is endlessly generative.
—Hiram Pérez, "You Can Have My Brown Body and Eat It, Too!"

In *Their Dogs Came with Them,* acclaimed Chicana writer Helena María Viramontes situates a gender variant genderqueer Chicanx person in the context of a surreal urban nightmare within a dystopic Chicanx past. Using inassimilable genders in a tale of Chicanx history contributes to the making of an archive of queer brown lives—and deaths—that negate the assimilationist progress script imposed on ethnic groups. Viramontes's fiction offers the potential to imagine Chicanx futures from a place of broken ground, from an unredeemed past or nonredemptive history. Demonstrating that Chicanx time has always been queer, Viramontes renders a version of Chicanx history that refuses to adhere to a dominative linear progression of assimilation. *Their Dogs Came with Them* looks to a queer Chicanx past as a space not only of loss but also as a persistent possibility that can accompany loss.

The novel maps the lives of four Chicanas navigating personal and political unrest in East L.A. in the tumultuous 1960s and 1970s.[1] One of the intertwining narratives follows a masculine Chicana gang member—Turtle—struggling to survive as a queerly gendered racialized subject on the streets of a devastated urban landscape. The dystopic tenor of the novel not only queers

Chicanx historical memory but also prompts the question of when and where there has ever been a time and place for Chicanxs and Latinxs in the United States.

Of Viramontes's earlier writing, Raul Villa contends that the author's use of the freeway as spatial metaphor in her fiction signals "Viramontes's own authorial struggle to discursively render the consequences of East Los Angeles' social-geographic subordination into usable, transmittable community knowledge through the medium of her fiction" (130). Feminist theorist Norma Alarcón, in "Making 'Familia' from Scratch," has read Viramontes's writing alongside Cherríe Moraga's to consider the construction of what Alarcón refers to as split subjectivities within their creative works. In *Feminism on the Border: Chicana Gender Politics and Literature*, Sonia Saldívar-Hull provides an insightful analysis of Viramontes's work as "utilizing a profoundly moving Chicana vernacular in the service of subaltern political aesthetics" and exemplifying a mode of enacting "transfrontera" feminism (125). Viramontes describes her own ongoing project as a writer as one of breaking down borders (Shea 41). Of the ongoing controversy over the xenophobic U.S. attempt to control the flow of Mexican immigrants by erecting a "border fence," Viramontes says that "I'd like to think that I am dismantling it, one word at a time." One of the ways Viramontes dismantles borders is by including queerly gendered characters in her fiction and emphasizing how queer Chicanxs have been an integral part of Chicanx history.

In this latest installment in Viramontes's corpus, the author turns her attention back to an eruptive time in Latinx L.A. Told from multiple perspectives, the narrative contains slippery chronologies and a spiraling timeline that zooms back and forth between perspectives and plots. The narrative deals with difficult themes of Chicanx experience without providing any entirely hopeful redemption or a happy ending. Moments of fantastical absurdity and frequent shifts across plot lines create a sense of uncertain location in time and space, fashioning an unstable world in which the characters face various types of displacement, loss, abandonment, violation, madness, and extreme loneliness. Through the disorientations produced by Viramontes's formal and narrative risk taking, characters become unmoored from any sense of safety, home, or self.

The novel features several young Chicanas in the 1960s, so readers might expect a bildungsroman following the coming-of-age of emerging players in the Chicano movement or perhaps an immigrant tale of upward mobility in striving for the American Dream. Or, with a queerly gendered character playing a major role, readers might expect a queer coming-out narrative. Viramontes upsets those expectations, instead providing a complex portrait of what Chicanidad looks like when loss is not redeemed. *Their Dogs Came with Them* does not turn away from the hard realities that existed alongside the political and social gains of the movimiento. Here, people do not triumph over oppression, violence does not cease, people wander the streets hungry, and struggling young people cannot transform the conditions of their lives.

Many critics have written about Viramontes's earlier works, particularly *The Moths and Other Stories,* and a growing body of criticism has begun to engage with her most recent novel. From an ecocritical perspective, Hsuan L. Hsu discusses how Viramontes's novel uses the metaphor of the L.A. freeway project, with its attendant destruction of long-standing Latino neighborhoods, to depict urbanization as a form of environmental racism. In *Profane & Sacred,* Bridget Kevane analyzes *Their Dogs Came with Them* by emphasizing what she describes as an interplay of the secular and spiritual. In *Latino Los Angeles in Film and Fiction: The Cultural Production of Social Anxiety,* Ignacio López-Calvo compares Viramontes's novel to works such as Luis J. Rodriguez's *The Republic of East L.A.* and other cultural productions that interrogate "the effect of urban redevelopment projects on the Chicano community" (López-Calvo 21). Gabriella Gutiérrez y Muhs's edited anthology *Rebozos de Palabras: An Helena María Viramontes Critical Reader,* offers a rich collection of critical readings by scholars Mary Pat Brady, Juanita Heredia, and Aldo Ulisses Reséndiz Ramírez. Thinking through the novel's feminist critique of the politics of spatial violences, Brady makes an important point when she reminds us that "it is not just people who have been displaced by the demands of a rescaled Los Angeles—it is the vast networks of affiliations and place-linked memories that have been ripped away" (178). Brady says that "[i]n giving us one dense portrait of East Los Angeles after another, Viramontes argues against the inhumanity and reductive aggression of the spatial rationalization inherent to the scaffold imagination. Spatial rationality works as a kind of crime" (178). Adding to these varied critical approaches, we can tune in to the intricacies of how Viramontes reconstructs an acutely devastating time in U.S. Latinx history. Informed by a similar concern with the relation between literary expression and social justice, my queer reading of the novel takes up the question of what the presence of genderqueer or queerly gendered bodies does for the telling of Chicanx histories.

Drawing on Jack Halberstam's notion of "queer time" (*In a Queer Time and Place* 1), I suggest that Viramontes's blurring of gender brings into sharp relief the untimeliness of nonnormativity that intersects in the genderqueer brown body. Conventional straight time has it that people grow up, go to college, get a job, get married, and have kids. When people rearrange or reject this order, the state gets anxious about how to keep people in line with straight time and its linear alignment with the dominant capitalist life cycle of consumption, which tends to be patterned according to such assumed life stages. To subvert this dominant paradigm of a lifetime, argues Halberstam, is to become a "queer subject" (9). A queer subject is one who manages to "live outside the logic of capital accumulation" (10). This does not necessarily mean just queer-identified people "but also those people who live without financial safety nets, without homes, without jobs, outside the organizations of time and space that have been established for the purposes of protecting the rich few from everyone else" (10).

As Juana María Rodríguez suggests in *Queer Latinidad*, "'Queer' is not simply an umbrella term that encompasses lesbians, bisexuals, gay men, two-spirited people, and transsexuals; it is a challenge to constructions of heteronormativity" (24). Such challenges in the Chicanx contexts of Viramontes's novel can be indexed as temporal. Viramontes's characters live lives full of disruptions and crises exacerbated by the structural and daily violences they experience as racialized queer subjects. By situating Chicanxs in a "queer time and place," Viramontes's narrative illustrates how linearity, reproduction, and heteronormativity are perpetually disrupted and undone in accounting for the alternative lived experiences of queer people and other nonnormative, marginalized subjects.

While Viramontes's writing does not typically get taken up under the rubric of queer Chicanx fiction, the acclaimed Chicana author has written queer subjects into the Chicanx historical imagination. The novel's deployment of genderqueerness and semblances thereof interrupt a "straight" reading of what might otherwise be considered a heteronormative Chicanx novel. In this vein, Viramontes's mobilization of gender and sexual ambiguities and nonlinear time resonates with Arturo Islas's complexly perverse, multigenerational homoeroticisms that inform his familial desert tales or with the cruising, nonreproductive time of erotic subcultures in John Rechy's early work. Similarly, Viramontes's novel contributes to Chicana literature that queers time, such as Emma Pérez's *Forgetting the Alamo: Or, Blood Memory,* casting Chicana lesbianas into the center of disruptive historical moments in Chicanx histories.

Their Dogs Came with Them interweaves the narratives of four young Chicanas marginalized within their own communities during the volatile decade. The protagonists include Ermila, a student at Garfield High School; Tranquilina, the daughter of Christian missionaries; Ana, a young professional caring for her schizophrenic brother Ben; and Turtle, a homeless gang member who lives her life on the streets passing as a man. Each of these characters attempts to navigate a world filled with the pervasive threat of violence. The queerly gendered character of Turtle provides a key to reading Viramontes's project in that Turtle's story of genderqueerness, homelessness, displacement, and violence resonates with the version of Chicanx history that Viramontes is trying to tell.

Of the four protagonists, Turtle, as an illegible genderqueer character, becomes the most marginalized, the most displaced, and the most disconnected. Turtle is also the character who does not survive. In a book about the losses of Chicanx history, it is Turtle who is ultimately irrevocably lost. Via the queerly gendered Turtle, Viramontes tells a much more broken version of Chicanx history than one might expect from a novel set in a Chicanx time often depicted as full of a hopeful, sí se puede political sentiment. Constructing a 1960s pseudo-historical Chicanx fiction with the genderqueer Turtle as a main axis, the novel rejects any romantic notions of a nostalgic Chicanx past. As a Chicanx subject without a home, real or imagined, Turtle embodies the difficulty of claiming a unified Chicanx consciousness, or an imaginary past Aztlánian homeland that all Chicanxs can rely on as a hopeful symbol of their collective future survival. The figure of the genderqueer Chicanx thus renders Chicanx history into a rather queer time and place, one in which the queer brown body figures prominently.

Displacement in the novel—especially for the queerly gendered Turtle—is never a choice; it is always a violent disruption, sudden and uncontrollable. Viramontes's portrayal of Mexican East L.A. in the 1960s provides a landscape for interrogating contemporary politics of spatial control and dislocation, particularly through the ambiguously gendered gang member Turtle. The narrative begins with a child watching an old woman pack up the contents of her home, which is about to be demolished by bulldozers.[2] The old woman cautions the child: "Pay attention. . . . [D]isplacement will always come down to two things: earthquakes or earthmovers" (8). A presumed rabies pandemic causes the city to rationalize placing East L.A. on curfew and in quarantine, using roadblocks to monitor people's movements. At the checkpoints, residents must present identification papers or risk brutal treatment by the specialized police force called the Quarantine Authority (Q.A.). The fictional events recall a time when Chicanx and Latinx neighborhoods experienced even more extreme policing of their everyday movements during times of mass ethnic uprising. The Q.A. seeks out Chicanxs as illegible queer subjects deserving to be surveilled and quarantined.

Viramontes confirms that the novel's partly autobiographical portrayal of the violent policing of Chicanx bodies by armed police patrols was part of her experience growing up in East Los Angeles. Her description of restricted mobility through the barrios of Los Angeles also brings to mind the militarized policing of the border that tries to separate Mexico from the United States: "I remember when we had curfews. We felt like criminals. We literally had to stop at points where we were asked where we were going, and what we were doing. We were trying to go into our own homes! Into our own neighborhoods!" (Mermann-Jozwiak and Sullivan 84). The tactic of using curfews and fences to control the movement of people of color in Los Angeles can be traced to crucial moments such as the Zoot Suit Riots of the 1940s, the Watts Riots of 1965, the school walkouts during the 1968 Chicano School Blowouts, the Chicano Moratorium of 1970, and the 1992 Los Angeles civil unrest following the acquittal of Los Angeles Police Department officers responsible for the beating of Rodney King. Before and during the Chicano movement in particular, Chicanxs and Latinxs in East L.A. neighborhoods were routinely monitored and harassed as they passed through checkpoints, similar to the immigration checkpoints operated by the Immigration and Naturalization Service and now by the Department of Homeland Security.

Of interest to Viramontes is how the Los Angeles police force has had a history of violence targeted at Chicanxs and people of color, particularly poor and marginalized people such as those depicted in the novel. Turtle, as Chicanx and genderqueer, becomes particularly vulnerable under the surveillance of a time curfew. The curfew restricts the mobility of all residents of Turtle's predominantly Chicanx working-class and poor barrio in order to isolate those subjects deemed especially suspicious or dangerous. As an unemployed queer Chicanx living on the streets, Turtle is precisely the improper subject who cannot make it home in time. Turtle has no fixed home to serve as a refuge during curfew and thus repeatedly becomes marked as someone who is out of time.

Throughout the narrative, Viramontes draws connections between the Spanish conquest of indigenous peoples in the Americas and the drastic urbanization of twentieth-century East L.A., particularly the mid-twentieth-century demolition of working-class Chicanx neighborhoods in order to pave the way for the modern freeway system. As Mary Pat Brady notes, "Repeating patterns all over Los Angeles, thriving neighborhoods made up of Mexican Americans were dismantled and displaced to spur an economic growth cycle that would largely exclude them" (93). Through the homeless character of Turtle, Viramontes focuses her attention on the poorest of the poor among the perpetually displaced Chicanx in East L.A.

The character Turtle begins living on the streets as a man after her brother Luis is drafted to serve in the Vietnam War and her family rejects her. As a member of her brother's street gang, Turtle seeks to survive in a gang culture that values and depends on violent masculinities. While the author describes Turtle as "androgynous," a more apt description would be ambiguously gendered, because Turtle is sometimes referred to as a woman and sometimes as a man but does not rely on terms such as "lesbiana," "maricona," "gay," or any other identity categories oft associated with queer Chicanx culture. Turtle's marginalized and unreadable body serves as both shelter and threat. Although we never ultimately find out how Turtle identifies, Turtle's queerness hovers as a ghostly possibility throughout the narrative.

While she is not identified explicitly as queer, Turtle's gender expression is certainly queer in that it reveals the inadequacy of the gender binary to place Turtle. Performing masculinity is, for Turtle, a matter of survival. Turtle's masculinity affords her a kind of shelter on the streets in that she can avoid the physical harassment directed at vulnerable women in street life. More than once, men on the street accost Turtle when they realize that she is a woman. Turtle tries to hide her body in her bulky jacket and clothing in order to appear ominously tough and masculine. This strategy provides her with a semblance of freedom of mobility as she moves through the barrio alone at night trying to find a place to sleep. In the end, however, her masculine appearance, and in particular her appearance as a Chicanx man, endangers her when the cops perceive her to be dangerous.

Turtle's physical presence suggests that she desires to present herself as a masculine-bodied person. She wears baggy men's clothes and a bulky leather jacket and is proud of emphasizing her physical size: "Turtle was large, and her mother had once said her largeness was bequeathed from a father they called Frank, though his real name was Francisco" (19). At one point, Turtle fondly remembers wearing her father's T-shirts when she was a little girl of eight years old (18). Her size becomes a matter of import when she lives on the streets of East L.A., where an imposing physical appearance can be an asset: "Her size gave the impression that Turtle was all muscle, a birthmark of luck in a neighborhood where might makes right" (20).

Early in the narrative, we learn how Turtle receives her nickname upon initiation into her brother's gang: "The name was her *For Real* one. She had been christened Turtle—always and por vida till death do us part—when she joined the McBride Boys with Luis Lil Lizard hasta la muerte. The two were known as half-and-half of the cold-blooded Gamboas" (16). Receiving an ambiguously gendered nickname serves as a rite of passage from a girl's childhood into a masculine gender expression on the streets. Turtle's christening marks her fellowship with her brother and their gang, cementing her identity as "one half of the cold-blooded Gamboas," binding her to a life of enforced violent masculinity.

Turtle moves cautiously through the streets, listening to her surroundings and the people she passes on the street more often than she speaks, and she carries a tool for a weapon: "she . . . slipped the large Workman screwdriver into the back pocket of her khakis, all the while listening. Hunger became unbearable, and she ambled to the end of the alley" (17). Turtle's masculinity allows her to hide and have a sense of mobility on the streets. This mobility is limited, and her masculinity is constructed through the particulars of the material conditions she faces. She does not have the money to buy a gun, so she carries a screwdriver for protection. She does not have money for food and has no family to feed her any longer, so her time on the streets is occupied with looking for something to eat.

While wandering the streets, Turtle catches sight of herself in a store window and imagines herself with a freshly shaved head: "In another life, Turtle had kept her head finely shaved, razor-skinned scalp shining. But as the days living on the streets turned into weeks, her hair had grown out unevenly, and she looked coffee-stained like an old kitchen sink. The studs stapled on the curves of her ears at first to disguise the Turtle in her but later to disguise the Antonia in him no longer had the glint of steel" (21). Poverty keeps Turtle from expressing the masculinity that she imagines might be available to her.

As the narrative tracks Turtle's displacement, it also empha-sizes the significance of the place of Los Angeles. In particular, the action follows characters through demolition zones and construc-tion zones along the newly constructed L.A. freeways. Using the landscape as palimpsest to be excavated from urban ruins, Vira-montes writes into the landscape people who have always been there but were seemingly invisible. Turtle first appears waking up alone in an alley after sleeping there all night: "Turtle perspired and waited, feeling the warm air vent against her leather jacket. Daylight slowly whittled away a new morning. She stretched her cramped legs, one and then the other, and slugged her thighs to arouse her muscles, make her legs spark into a run if need be" (16). She thinks she hears someone say her name, so she looks around and wonders whether she is being pursued by her own McBride Boys gang, by the rival Lote M Boys gang, or by the Quarantine Authority that monitors the streets.

As Viramontes leads us through Turtle's barrio streets in East Los Angeles, parallels between Turtle's dangerous street life and her brother Luis's dangerous life as a soldier in the Vietnam War emerge: "Patrol sirens and gunshot reports of the helicopters shot through her thin veil of sleep, and she had dreamt of Luis Lil Liz-ard crouching in the jungle somewhere in 'Nam, clinging to an army-issued rifle, his fingers trembling just as hers had been" (17). Likening the embattled, impoverished conditions of East L.A. to the war zone, Viramontes emphasizes the precariousness of the queerly gendered body in the masculine gang culture.

The various story lines that have been running parallel throughout the novel suddenly converge in a mass pileup in the end, all centered around Turtle. After her gang forces her into physically attacking a young boy, Turtle is shot by the police. Tranquilina, the daughter of Christian missionaries, who has only met Turtle once, tries to stop the police from shooting Turtle by screaming, "We'rrrre not doggggs!" (324). The attempt to protect Turtle comes too late, and Turtle faces the police shooters alone and vulnerable. Turtle's narrative ends abruptly and brutally, with her dead body twisted and bleeding on the street. Just as she had been rendered invisible, she is rendered silent: "Turtle's lips weighted down to muteness" (324). Her final thought is of her brother and the dismal wisdom he had offered her: "Luis Lil Lizard had once told her that them two lived in a stay of execution" (324). With a violent life full of displacement and a seemingly inevitable violent death, being gunned down by police on the street, Turtle signifies the queer Chicanx body marked for erasure by racialized and gendered violence.

Tranquilina's insistence that she and Turtle and the other Chicanxs are "not dogs" recalls the epigraph that opens the novel. The epigraph quotes a passage from Miguel Léon-Portilla's *The Broken Spears: The Aztec Account of the Conquest of Mexico.* In the account, Aztec (Mexica) people describe the arrival of Spanish conquistadors and their packs of trained canines: "Their dogs came with them, running ahead of the column. They raised their muzzles high; they lifted their muzzles to the wind. They raced on before with saliva dripping from their jaws" (*Their Dogs Came with Them* n.p.). The dogs that accompanied the conquistadores were especially trained to rip flesh, becoming yet another weapon to destroy the bodies of the colonized, particularly the gender nonconforming. As Deborah Miranda notes, the Spanish colonizers often used dogs specifically to punish nonconforming queerly gendered indigenous bodies (256). In *Their Dogs Came with Them,* the Quarantine Authority serves the function of the conquistadores and their attack dogs, terrorizing barrio residents such as Turtle as they try to move through their own familiar streets. Turtle experiences multiple temporalities, presently moving through the L.A.

streets while haunted by the persistent ghosts of colonization—in the form of the Spanish colonizers' attack dogs. Turtle, as queerly racialized, becomes subjected to state-sponsored tactics for recolonizing Chicanxs.

In the world of *Their Dogs Came with Them*, Turtle exists in a suspended state of loss, of losing her brother Luis to the U.S. war against Vietnam, of witnessing the bulldozers tear down her barrio. At one point, she contemplates the erasure of her barrio as she literally reads the writing on the wall: "She could read, Turtle wasn't stupid. The cross-outs, tags, new gang emblems trashed all over McBride's graffiti on the walls of the bridge—all bad news" (217).

The blurring of barrio street life with war zone imagery makes it difficult to discern whether the ticking object Turtle hears is a bomb or a clock that marks time as the barrio is disappearing. As Turtle reads the rival gang's graffiti painted over her own, she contemplates not just her fear of her barrio disappearing but also her fear of her own disappearance. She imagines the rival gang's tags as "a dispatch announcing erasure" (217). This "dispatch announcing erasure" is a callback to the image of the pack of dogs running ahead of the Spanish conquerors in the initial image of the book's epigraph. Thus, Turtle stands witness to yet another series of conquests that have shaped Chicanx queer experience. This time, however, rather than a foreign imperial invasion, the colonization takes the form of an internal colonization by other Chicanxs. In the scene described above, Turtle lists her brother and herself among those to be erased. As she laments how Luis is "erased" by the state's war machine rather than the street's war machine, she lists her own name among those who may inevitably be lost to the violence of the streets.

Turtle also experiences the loss of her family. After Luis is drafted, Turtle's family begins to reject her more and more for her manly looks. Without her brother at her side, Turtle becomes vulnerable to the harsh scrutiny of her queer appearance: "'What's with the shaved head?' Aunt Mercy asked Amá, though Turtle stood right in front of her. Aunt Mercy had a way of excluding people from a conversation. She had a way of making people like

Turtle feel invisible though they were maybe two feet from her" (167). Turtle's aunt then refers to her as "malflora." While "malflora" literally means "bad flora" or "bad flower," it is a slang term for "lesbian," synonymous with tortillera or jota, and may be considered more offensive than "lesbiana." The term is a variation of "manflora," which can be used to describe a masculine woman or an effeminate man, evoking the association of women's masculinity with both supposedly failed masculinity and supposedly inadequate femininity.[3] Turtle's Aunt Mercy refers to Turtle as "malflora" without addressing her directly, making Turtle feel "invisible" in her own home among her own family. After this incident, Turtle resolves to leave her home. "The word 'malflora' sounded so sad to Turtle, it was a word you shouldn't be left alone with" (168). Nonetheless, Turtle takes to the L.A. streets on her own.

Although the novel includes a queer character, it does not focus on the sexuality of that queer character; instead, through the character of Turtle, Viramontes depicts the despairing possibilities that can occur to an individual whose in-between body and underclass status compound the struggle to survive at the most basic level. Turtle decides to move through the world as a man, wanting to be read by others as a man. However, Turtle's gender expression is not necessarily queer in the sense of being sexually queer. Turtle's sexuality is not directly addressed, and her physical gender presentation is inextricably intertwined with her desire to belong to the neighborhood gang, the McBride Boys. Turtle's gender expression serves as her street mask, her shell or protective layer that keeps her from being read as a woman and therefore a vulnerable target in street life. We do not ever learn whether Turtle is indeed queer or whether she experiences sexual feelings at all.

Just as Viramontes subverts a queer coming-out narrative, she resists the conventions of a Chicanx coming-to-consciousness narrative. The novel subverts the expectations of coming to social consciousness literature or social protest literature of the Chicano movement, instead showing those left behind or unaffected by the movement of the time. While hanging out near a bus stop, Turtle observes a young Chicano's obliviousness to the people around him: "To the left of the mailbox, a young pimply man read a brick of a paperback and didn't even look up to notice the woman who sat at the bus bench and rustled a grocery bag between them." She passes judgment on the young man, suggesting that he is self-absorbed or disillusioned: "Turtle guessed the scar-faced man was a Che Guevara wannabe, a brown beret flopped on his head like the mural on the wall of the Ramona Gardens housing projects. Who did he think he was fooling?" (17).

Despite being in the same barrio as this Brown Beret, there exists a cavernous social distance between Turtle's world and the resistance movements being organized under the rubric of the Chicano movement. Unlike the winning heroic narratives that position the Chicanx protagonist as an agent of social change, *Their Dogs Came with Them* shows the potentially disastrous consequences of not having access to organized community other than street gangs. Turtle does not seem to recognize the actual group or social movement associated with the man's brown beret (though she does reference the Latin American revolutionary Che Guevara), although she guesses by his appearance and behavior that he aspires to radical political aims. But his revolutionary status strikes Turtle as purely academic, ineffectual, and lonely.

For a coming-to-consciousness narrative, one possible narrative strategy would have been to include a Chicanx activist as a protagonist. That strategy has been pursued by several Chicanx authors, such as Américo Paredes in his novel *George Washington Gomez* and Alicia Gaspar de Alba in her mystery novel *Desert Blood*, in which a Chicana lesbian academic activist leads a community's investigation into the femicides in El Paso/Juarez. As in Paredes's novel, such a strategy affords the reader the opportunity to venture into experiences of the emergent activist facing choices around whether and how to become a "voice of the people."

Viramontes sets up a similar readerly expectation via the chapter on Ermila and the high school students who bristle at the inequitable treatment they receive at Garfield High School, the site of the Chicanx school walkouts in the 1960s. However, Viramontes only flirts with the possibility that Ermila and her comrades might become Chicanx activists; instead, she repeatedly bucks that expectation by having the girls be more drawn to forming a women's street gang. In doing so, Viramontes subverts the generic conventions of building an individual Chicanx hero/heroine in favor of showing the material pressures and social conditions that give rise to gang formation among Chicanx youth in urban barrios.

Viramontes uses the figure of the ambiguously gendered queer racial body, in the character of Turtle, to subvert the conventions of the American coming-out narrative and the ethnic coming-to-consciousness identity struggle, focusing her narrative around erasure and loss rather than personal or political triumphs. Turtle imagines herself as a man and as physically masculine and then struggles with what those attributes mean to her socially. Aligning oneself with a masculinity that equates strength with the violent expression of coercive power over others leaves Turtle alone, abandoned, and victimized by the police force as well as by her fellow gang members. Her aberrant body finds no home in the brotherhood of the McBride Boys, no welcoming home in her biological family of origin, and no safe place on the streets to become the man she imagines herself to be. After Turtle, high on drugs given to her by her gang, stabs and kills a young man marked by her gang, an alarmed passerby tries to interrogate Turtle about her motive: "Why? the woman asked Turtle, and kept asking." Turtle, however, cannot herself make sense of the senselessness of her situation: "'Why' was not a word that meant something to Turtle." Turtle concludes that perhaps the earlier version of Turtle never really existed: "Why? Because a tall girl named Antonia never existed, because her history held no memory. Why? Go ask another" (324). Turtle might momentarily recognize herself as what Antonio Viego refers to as a "dead subject," marked as lacking and powerless—a paradoxically knowable entity considered nonexistent—within the American popular imaginary.[4] The police force perceives her as a brown-bodied man, which translates as not only a dangerous body but also a dispensable one. However, if we read Turtle's death, while tragic, as a radical opening that demands imagining alternatives for queer Chicanxs, we can follow Viramontes's implicit lead into expansive possibilities. The trick becomes for queer Chicanxs to challenge the state in radical and productive ways without being subject to punishment for it. Rather than an entirely dead subject, Turtle becomes a ghost that haunts Chicanx consciousness, waiting for us to place an offering upon the altar of never forgetting.

In a moment of foreshadowing, Turtle gazes upon a dead female dog on the street and refuses to extend sympathy for the dog not having survived the violence of the streets: "[A] bloodied dog's carcass from last night's search littered the street, ground raw into the pavement by car tires. . . . It must have been female, Turtle judged, because purple droopy teats fell to one side. Black veils of flies swarmed every inch of flesh. Sorry, bitch, she thought, I didn't make the rules. The flies hung tight together, even in the rain" (29). In Turtle's cold reaction to the dead dog on the street, Viramontes critiques the brutality of a violent ethic. Viramontes reflects on her exploration of violence horizontally inflicted by the oppressed on other oppressed people: "The impetus of the novel was that I was trying to understand why there was so much brown-on-brown violence. Why are we killing ourselves, and killing ourselves with such brutality? . . . [S]o how did we become dogs then? If we are treated like dogs, we become dogs" (Mermann-Jozwiak and Sullivan 85). Although Turtle fails to explicitly make the connection between the dog's ominous fate and her own brutal existence, she does apologize to the dog and distance herself from those who "make the rules." Turtle's reference to the female dog as "bitch" reminds us that Turtle has not had access to the solidarity of women.

The fend-for-yourself attitude that seeing the dog's dead body evokes in Turtle mirrors the survival logic required within the material conditions of trying to live on the streets. Critic Sonia Saldívar-Hull discusses not only the brutality but also the colonizing logic of the barrio in Viramontes's "Paris Rats in L.A." (which served as a seed story for the novel *Their Dogs Came with Them*): "Instead of the media oversimplifications of barrio as gang-violence war zone, she [Viramontes] presents barrio as township, barrio as home, and its young men and women in gangs" (155).

Saldívar-Hull goes on to say that "[a]dmittedly, the gang ethic is violent, but this political narrative gives us the reasons (or *a* reason) for the violence. She offers us insights into how our children, our young women and men, are tracked to lives on the margins, on the borders, of the United States" (155). She notes that "Viramontes gives a name, a face, and ultimately humanity to people whom the dominant group prefers to keep anonymous, sinister, and therefore easier to kill on the street or to disappear into the labyrinth of the U.S. prison system" (155). As Saldívar-Hull astutely observes, Viramontes constructs worlds that are certainly "no Aztlán, the mythical homeland of the Aztec natives and the utopian dreamland of the Chicano nationalists of the 1960s and 1970s" (159). The L.A. barrio life portrayed by Viramontes depicts subjects for whom "Aztlán does not exist" (159). If Antonia never existed, neither did her potential history or an imagined Aztlánian homeland. Turtle has no usable Chicanx past to recall and no access to a queer history with which to insert herself as an imaginable and legible subject of experience.

Turtle and the other characters in *Their Dogs Came with Them* are indeed far removed from the imagined unity of an Aztlán homeland or the sense of shared political impetus that Aztlán provides. Lázaro Lima comments on the construction of Aztlán in the Chicanx imaginary: "Indeed it was the paucity of narrative models that made the Chicanx movement found a public identity centered on Mexico's indigenous heritage and the greatness of the Aztec civilization through the invocation of Aztlán, the mythic homeland of the Aztec in the southwestern United States" (17). As Lima claims, "Aztlán created a logic of presence that grounded Chicano experience and being *in* the United States, thereby making Chicanos heirs to an indigenous historical tradition that antedated the Anglo-American presence in the country" (17). Lima describes the construction of Aztlán as a Chicano homeland as "a cultural nationalist assault on American cultural amnesia" and argues that Latino as a "crisis identity becomes historical in order to assert a continuous presence, resisting the false notion that *all* Latinos are newcomers to the United States" (17). In Lima's estimation, "the racializations of Latinos and the presumptive grounds by with [sic] they have been constructed almost exclusively as extra-nationals in the public sphere—from the Mexican-American War to the present—have sustained and implicitly sanctioned a 'tiered democracy of bodies' where certain national bodies matter more than others" (169). For Viramontes, writing Turtle into the historical fiction of East L.A. asserts the historical presence of the marginalized, unrecognizably genderqueer Chicana body into the narrative of Chicanidad.

Regarding the role of Aztlán in understanding her queer identity as a Chicanx, Moraga, in her "Queer Aztlán" essay in *The Last Generation*, asserts that "Aztlán gave language to a nameless anhelo [ache] inside" her (225). Turtle has no language to name her ache other than "hunger" and no language to name her experience as a Chicanx, much less as a queer or a genderqueer Chicana, other than malflora. Additionally, Turtle has no queer or lesbian community or context in which she can even begin to make sense to herself as queer. Turtle becomes like the turtle image evoked in Moraga's *Loving in the War Years* (125), in which Moraga asserts that no one wants to be made so vulnerable: "Nobody wants to be made to feel the turtle with its underside all exposed, just pink and folded flesh" (125). While Moraga uses this image to describe her desire to become butch and to feel less vulnerable, it suggests a penetrability of the feminine body that amounts to death for a masculine woman who does not want to be made to feel exposed or vulnerable. In fact, Turtle does not want to feel at all and is surprised at the pain she feels upon death: "Stunned, Turtle looked bewildered and then felt a sticky ball of grit push from between her swollen lips. . . . Only the pain, which overwhelmed, surprised her" (Viramontes, *Their Dogs Came with Them* 324). In some ways a cloak of masculinity serves Turtle well within a Chicanx space, but once she moves out of that space to a larger urban sphere, her body gets read by the police as a dangerous person of color. Turtle's racialized Chicanx and gender-nonconforming body disrupts the police state's ability to mark and read subjects as belonging and is met with a violent response from the police.

Upon Turtle's death the novel ends abruptly, with the religious Tranquilina walking toward the police, who still have their guns drawn. The ambiguous ending leaves us without a known path for Tranquilina and the others; we do not know whether the police shoot Tranquilina as well. As this tale of Chicanx barrio history closes in a queer time and place with Turtle's loss and no hope for a certain future, Viramontes resists utopic visions of either past or present, disrupting heternormative versions of Chicanx history.

Unclear time serves as the modus operandi for this novel, as the focus shifts across plot lines and back and forth through time unexpectedly. By showing the urban decay of 1960s East L.A. and referencing the arrival of the Spanish into ancient Mexico, it becomes uncertain which moment of colonization the characters are experiencing. Additionally, relationships among characters are not neatly categorizable into a traditional nuclear family structure or single-family household dwellings or even into immediate and extended family. Neighborhood children spend significant time with elderly neighbors, making it unclear where the kids actually live. Turtle has flashbacks to living at home with parents and her brother and being visited by aunts and uncles, but Turtle spends most of the novel homeless, trying to survive on the streets. At one point she contemplates going to a neighbor for help but chooses not to because she fears rejection for her masculine appearance and for her gang association.

Turtle is cast to the other side, beyond the sheltering border of family, gang, barrio. Her narrative ends abruptly and brutally, with Turtle's dead body twisted and bleeding on the street. Viramontes effectively uses the genderqueer figure to turn the turtle over onto its back to look at its fleshy parts and how they can be hurt. She exposes the soft underbelly of Chicanx history, revealing what happens in the interstices when people are not becoming queer or becoming free. Viramontes focuses on in-between bodies, in-between places that are and are not East L.A., during in-between times that are and are not Chicanx history.

While I have not seen Viramontes's historical fiction listed among the banned ethnic studies books in Arizona,[5] I suggest that it is as daring and provocative as some of the foundational Chicanx studies texts that have been targeted for levying smart critiques of systemic U.S. Chicanxphobia. As queered historical fiction, the novel certainly contributes to the sociopolitical project of socially conscious Chicanx literature as well as ethnic studies. It reminds us that one reason the project of ethnic studies—and its attendant literature—threatens the white supremacist establishment is not simply because it focuses on one group over another but, more important, because it refuses to sanitize histories of violence and exclusion perpetrated against racial-ethnic minoritarian groups. In imagining a narrative of East Los Angeles history, Viramontes could have taken a triumphalist approach that showed only positive portrayals of Chicanxs making it against all odds. However, Viramontes's novel refuses to play nice and paint over the devastating material realities that have informed the Chicanx lives she depicts.

The novel does share some commonalities with canonized Chicanx literature in terms of dealing with historical colonization, forced migration, family bonds, and other themes. But on the whole, *Their Dogs Came with Them* does not fit squarely within dominant conventions of common Chicanx fictional genres. This is not a sprawling, multigenerational family saga. This is not an individual journey of coming-of-age or a collective voice of group identity formation. This is not a straightforward immigrant tale or migration tale. Is it not a return home, nor is it nostalgia for a pristine homeland. This is not realism, though it is gritty. This is not magical realism, though it flirts with the surreal. This is not a coming out, an exile, the making of an ethnic representative hero/ine.

These conventions of genre and artistic modes of cultural representation may have their place in the realm of Chicanx literary and cultural production, but Viramontes achieves something forceful by showing how Chicanx operates in yet another register. This is a fiction that considers what is means to be born "here" under the sign of U.S. American during a time of civil rights progress and promise and yet be cast out by various institutions, unrecognizable by common structures of racial-ethnic identity making. To be finally interpellated in the Althusserian sense, to be called into recognition as a subject of the state's machinery only when one has been hailed by a bullet.

Through this queer Chicanx fiction, Chicanxs continue to be constructed as inassimilable into the U.S. historical imaginary in that it is still not considered time for Chicanxs to be incorporated wholly as legitimate subjects of U.S. national meaning making. Affiliations with transnational migration, repeated border crossings, and internal colonization continue to trouble the U.S. misconception of immigration-cum-American as linear, as a one-way street of desire. Ethnic subjects who engage in conceptions of recursive time and shifting identities exceed the limits of U.S. American national identity and risk censure for appearing counterproductive, unruly, and untimely.

Viramontes's latest contribution to Chicanx literature makes use of gender variance and Chicanx untimeliness to demand an accounting of the dead. The tragic narrative suggests that if Chicanx literature, and perhaps one might argue Chicanx studies more broadly, has leaned heavily on the family unit, ethnic identity, and the nation-state as viable constructs, how might we imagine otherwise? Viramontes raises questions about what other forms of relationality, affiliation, and solidarity might be forged, particularly for gender variant Chicanx subjects. Through the specter of seemingly inevitable queer Chicanx death, Viramontes invites a radical reconsideration of the potential futures that Chicanxs might ascribe to, especially when the family fails us, the nation-state disenfranchises us, and the next neocolonizers bring their dogs with them.

3

Transing Chicanidad

> If we can become speaking subjects only by occupying legible
> nodes within institutional structures—that is, by having a name,
> performing a recognized demographic category, and so forth—we
> also reckon with the fact that we exceed every possible legible
> node…sometimes so much that the institution literally has
> no place for us, or violently *mis*-places, such subjectivities.
> —A. Finn Enke, *Transfeminist Perspectives*

In the essay "Chicana Lesbians: Fear and Loathing in the Chicano Community" in *Chicana Lesbians: The Girls Our Mothers Warned Us About*, Carla Trujillo contends that Chicanxs have historically perceived lesbians as threats. This lament has been widely expressed by Trujillo's literary peers Cherríe Moraga, Gloria Anzaldúa, and 1980s borderlands generation authors who struggled with whether their lesbian identity was at odds with their ethnic identity. Moraga's *Loving in the War Years: Lo Que Nunca Pasó Por Sus Labios* engages the struggles of being a mixed-race light-skinned Chicana, a lesbian, and a feminist. Anzaldúa's *Borderlands/La Frontera: The New Mestiza* grapples with historical erasure and recovery of Chicana experience, sexual violence against women, and forming feminist alliances across racial and ethnic differences. These representative borderlands generation texts are predominately concerned with what it means to be a Chicana lesbian disowned by

Chicanxs and what it means to be a feminist woman of color who is unseen by white feminists.

The Chicana lesbian in the borderlands, for both Anzaldúa and Moraga, has no home and must make her own psychic and cultural home out of the remains of her loss and out of what Anzaldúa refers to as her "own feminist architecture." In the final passage of Cherríe Moraga's mixed-genre text *Loving in the War Years*—a collection of essays, poems, and vignettes—the butch Chicana lesbian narrator says "En el sueño mi amor pregunta 'Dónde está tu río?' And I point to the middle of my chest" (145). When her lover asks her in a dream "Where is your river?" and the lesbiana points to the middle of her chest, to her body's core, or her corazón, she responds in a similar vein as the narrator of Gloria Anzaldúa's *Borderlands/La Frontera* faced with a similar question: Where is your border, where is your home/land? Anzaldúa's voice of the new mestiza responds that her home is "a vague and undetermined place." "Wherever I go," she says, "I carry home on my back" (43).

Chicana lesbian texts of the post-borderlands, however, suggest that it is not lesbianism, same-sex desire, or even sexuality in general but instead genderqueerness that poses greater challenges to the coherence of the Chicanx community and a shared Chicanx imaginary. Genderqueerness, because of its unreadability, ultimately poses a bigger threat to a Chicanx imaginary than same-sex desire. This shift in a Chicana lesbian feminist consciousness to privilege genderqueerness over queer sexuality is evident in the works of contemporary queer Chicana novelist Felicia Luna Lemus. Lemus's fiction signals a shift away from a borderlands consciousness that saw same-sex desire as the ultimate cultural taboo. While Lemus's texts do share some borderlands concerns in that they continue the borderlands project of imagining a place for lesbians and queers in Chicanx community, they also extend this cultural work by writing genderqueerness or nonnormative genders into the picture.

In Lemus's work, it is not just sexuality but also genderqueerness that becomes the next borderlands of Chicanx identity to be crossed, entered, negotiated, constructed, interrogated, and imagined. In Lemus's first novel, *Trace Elements of Random Tea Parties*, published by Seal Press in 2003, a Chicana dyke named Leti navigates adventures in love and family while being haunted by Weeping Woman, La Llorona of Mexican folk legend. Lemus's second novel, *Like Son*, published by Akashic Books in 2007, tells the story of Frank, who negotiates similar adventures in love and family as a female-to-male transgender person. Both of Lemus's narratives explore how nonnormative genders push the boundaries of sexuality beyond a straight/queer binary to include questions of gender expression.

Lemus's fiction considers the possibilities and binds of gender variance for Chicanxs and opens up a space for talking about the shifting and complex dynamics between race and ethnicity as well as between gender and sexuality in ways not necessarily taken up by many of her literary Chicana predecessors. Lemus's fiction complicates the issues of gender identity, gender expression, genderqueerness, and transgender identity, participating in a praxis of transing. In the introduction to the "Trans-" special issue of *Women's Studies Quarterly*, Susan Stryker, Paisley Currah, and Lisa Jean Moore state that "'[t]ransing,' in short, is a practice that takes place within, as well as across or between, gendered spaces. It is a practice that assembles gender into contingent structures of association with other attributes of bodily being, and that allows for their reassembly" (13). Through transing, Lemus's characters reassemble gender into a renegotiation with racialized Chicanidad.

In this process, Lemus's texts are not concerned with naming or locating themselves within a geopolitical, ethnic, psychological, or spiritual borderlands, as were Chicana lesbian texts of the 1980s and 1990s. Characters in Lemus's novels take a borderlands identity as a given, assumed or unquestioned, amounting to a mainstreamed, acceptable otherness. They then build multiple layers of identity, constructing hybrid subjectivities that cannot be fully located, especially by other Chicanxs.

While much Chicana literature has explored the oppositional dynamics of Chicanx versus Anglo, citizen versus immigrant-as-foreigner, working class versus middle and owning class, female versus male, and queer versus straight, Lemus adds to the matrices of identity and power by exploring what it means to be genderqueer versus normative as well as punkera/punk versus mainstream. Yvonne Yarbro-Bejarano states that Lemus's novel *Trace Elements of Random Tea Parties* emphasizes "alternative temporalities and kinship groupings" ("Queer Storytelling and Temporality in Trace Elements of Random Tea Parties by Felicia Luna Lemus" 73). In so doing, Lemus's fiction considers the possibilities and binds of genderqueerness for Chicanxs. Her work suggests that genderqueerness disrupts a sense of unified cultural wholeness in the Chicanx imaginary. But Lemus's work is not just about rupture; it is also about reclamation and recovery in that for Lemus's characters genderqueerness allows for reclaiming lost history and coming to terms with a collective Chicanx sense of lost wholeness.

Some of the Chicana lesbian anthologies and fictional works prior to Lemus's use the term "lesbian." Lemus, however, eschews the label "lesbian" altogether and tends to use "dyke" and "queer" interchangeably in her novels. Lemus's usage may reflect a historical shift away from "lesbian" and "gay" identities toward "queer" as a more common signifier. While Lemus does not use terms such as "genderqueer," "transsexual," or "transgender," her work nonetheless takes up these issues and identities as inherently bound up in queer Chicanx experience.

In the introduction to the 2002 anthology *GenderQueer: Voices from Beyond the Sexual Binary,* edited by Joan Nestle, Clare Howell, and Riki Wilchins, coeditor Wilchins offers a definition of genderqueerness that encompasses sex, gender, and sexuality: "In a society where femininity is feared and loathed, all women are genderqueer. In a culture where masculinity is defined by having sex with women and femininity by having sex with men, all gay people are gender queers" (12). Wilchins also notes that "whenever gender is mentioned, it is inevitably written down—and too often written off—as only transgender" (15). Drawing on Wilchins's generalized definition, I am using "genderqueer" to denote gender variant identities and expressions that seek to disrupt or transcend binaries or to resist gender norms.

In an interview of the author conducted by Michelle Tea, Lemus describes her project of representing and imagining genderqueer Chicanas. Tea says that when she first read Lemus's novel *Trace Elements of Random Tea Parties*, she was confused by all of the gender fluidity. In the novel, the protagonist Leti does not assume or adopt either a feminine or masculine gender expression and maintain it as though it were a fixed identity. Lemus offers that representing gender fluidity "was important to me also in terms of being Chicana" (Tea 178). Lemus goes on to say that "I don't know many androgynous Chicanas or anyone who plays that line quite like I see people of different ethnicities play it. People who are still very much in touch with their culture, who aren't more assimilated, they still play by the kind of old school rules of butch/femme. And I respect that. There's something about it culturally that works." Notably, Lemus relegates butch-femme to the past, where "old school rules" are at work. Lemus also associates butch-femme in Chicana culture with the lack of assimilation into mainstream white culture. The rules of butch-femme, then, become for Lemus markers of an ethnic authenticity, a sense of being "in touch" with one's culture. This positions butch-femme is traditional in Chicano culture, which potentially opens a way for anything outside the butch-femme paradigm to seem more assimilated and hence less Chicanx.

Leti's gender fluidity challenges gender norms among Chicanxs, queer and straight. Tea's question about the text speaks to how the narrative enacts gender fluidity by disrupting any expectations or assumptions of a gender binary. This shifting terrain of gender expressions makes the main character's gender unpredictable and unreadable by some around her.

In her fiction, Lemus explores what happens for Chicanxs outside of the butch-femme binary. Her challenge of the Chicana butch-femme binary emphasizes how butch-femme has become a marked point of reference for Chicana lesbians. Indeed, Moraga's autobiographical writings, particularly *Loving in the War Years*, contributed to the construction of butch-femme as a prevalent form of gender identities among Chicana lesbians. Moraga's literary persona as a Chicana butch looms large among the representative body of Chicana lesbian literature. Given such a literary legacy, Lemus's texts can be read as laments as well as celebratory representations of the (im)possibility of genderqueerness beyond butch-femme in Chicanidad. The unreadability of gendered subjects in Lemus's novels makes certain kinds of genderqueerness more out of place in Chicano culture than other kinds of lesbian genders. By focusing on versions of genderqueerness that do *not* work culturally, Lemus exposes how the cultural signs and systems that work and do not work get read, misread, or not read according to Chicanx understandings of normative genders.

If butch-femme, as Lemus claims, "works" culturally, it is because it is to some extent accepted, or acceptable, in Chicanx culture. Lemus's comment reveals how butch-femme can be viewed as homonormative among queers yet heteronormative within the context of traditional Chicano culture. But this acceptability of butch-femme can be at the expense of allowing other gender identities or expressions to flourish; unfortunately, butch-femme can render other forms of genderqueerness unreadable or unallowable. The idea that butch-femme entirely "works" in Chicano culture breaks down in Lemus's novels, however, in that the butch or genderqueer lesbians are rejected by or cast out of their families. How does butch-femme "work" if, in Lemus's texts, the butch or masculine woman or genderqueer is cast out of Chicano family and community? How does butch-femme "work," if the butch part of the equation is not accepted on its own? There is an elision that occurs culturally between the lesbian frame of reference and a genderqueerness frame of reference. Butch-femme is a lesbian gender system that is recognizable within a Chicano context either because of its assumed resemblance to heterosexual gender paradigms or perhaps because of lesbian cultural work to assert its meaning. But a butch alone, without being coupled with or associated as paired with a femme, is typically read as genderqueer before she is read as a lesbian or dyke. That is, a Chicana butch gets read as gender variant before she gets read as a lesbian. Any genderqueerness is suspect or rejected because it is presumed to be unacceptable and unreadable. Lemus's genderqueer protagonists are unreadable as either femme or butch, the only readable or discernible categories of gender expression deemed allowable for Chicana lesbians. And even within the tolerated binary of butch-femme, the feminine is considered socially acceptable, excluding the masculine woman, the butch, from what is allowed to be seen or expressed. Lemus incisively gets at the reality yet impossibility of women's masculinity and gender variance among queer Chicanxs.

The novel *Trace Elements of Random Tea Parties* privileges a working-class genderqueer Chicana dyke subjectivity, attempting to write this subject into an empowered position in the Chicanx imaginary. Yet, the text ultimately renders this Chicana dyke subject *unreadable* by mainstream Chicanxs, leaving her with alliances outside Chicanx culture but without a Chicano community. This move to position the genderqueer Chicana as liberated only outside of the Chicano community addresses the problematic of genderqueer subjectivity in relation to Chicanidad.

The novel uses two queer Chicana characters, Leti and Edith, to show how Chicana lesbians negotiate aspects of their identity and can make radically different choices around them. Leti, as the central figure in the text, becomes the focal point for the development of a particular kind of Chicana dyke identity deemed authentic; Edith's Chicana lesbian identity becomes discounted around the issue of class. Identity in this text is highly performative and centers around shared sexuality, gender expression, and class in ways that may privilege those aspects of identity *over* ethnicity, calling into question the notion that one's ethnicity is always central to one's identity. Furthermore, Lemus's narrative configures Chicana dyke identity as so extremely performative and fluid as to become constantly in transitio, and hence indefinable.

The protagonist, Leti, is a college-educated Chicana lesbian with a working-class background. Leti does not fret over what it means to be a Chicana. And once her character comes out as a lesbian early on in the novel, she does not have any notable identity struggles over her sexuality. It is Leti's genderqueerness that becomes the central aspect of her character's identity struggles. Leti and other characters in the novel push at the boundaries of traditional gender expression. Leti plays with gender expression by mixing feminine and masculine clothing and by referring to herself alternately as dyke, boy, boy-girl, femme, or princess. In one moment, Leti is wearing pearls and insists on calling herself "princess." Later, she dresses herself in what she refers to as "boy" clothes.

Throughout the narrative, Leti and her friends play with gender. This may involve dressing masculine or feminine, being androgynous, or combining these attributes. They move seemingly randomly along a gender expression continuum, engaging in what critic Jack Halberstam describes in *Female Masculinity* as "layering" (261), the practice of donning a layer of outer attire that signifies one's so-called "opposite" gender. Drag performers, for example, often engage in layering that does not try to fully "hide" another gender expressed by the body underneath. According to Halberstam, one who engages in this type of gender play through dress does not hide but instead reveals—by allowing all of the layers to show at once, making a genderqueer performance a way of exposing the ludicrous limitations of a binaristic gender system.

For Leti, this type of gender play becomes an integral part of how she moves through her queer world. Before going out to Crystal's, her favorite dyke bar, she carefully chooses her attire, pointing out that she wears her pearl choker "especially if [she] was going to Crystal's" (56). Leti indeed engages in this type of "layering" gender play and seems to revel in queering her gender not just by occasionally dressing masculine but also by mixing elements of masculine and feminine dress, causing all of her layers of gender expression to show at once.

A similar layering operates at the level of self-representation through the novel's language. Lemus portrays a fluidity of gender via a fluidity of language in the novel. Lemus's peculiar use of repetitive descriptions evokes a poetic device employed by the Mexica, or ancient Aztecs. In Nahuatl poetry renaming through repetition is common, as is the use of compound words and phrases such as in the term *xochicuicatl,* which translates to the compound "flower-song" (*flor y canto*) or, in a poem, referring to a hummingbird as "humming-bird, the emerald trembler" (Curl 4).[1] This repetition for emphasis is also a poetic strategy used by seventeenth-century Mexican poet Sor Juana Inés de la Cruz, known for her outspoken feminist critiques of Mexican social and religious institutions. In *Chicano Poetics: Heterotexts and Hybridities,* Alfred Arteaga associates Sor Juana's use of inverted repetitive phrases as a gendered chiasmus, a rhetorical device illustrative of the feminist resistance expressed in her work. In the case of Lemus, the redundant phrases occasionally use a part to describe a whole in the form of a metonymy or synecdoche but are more often descriptive or stylistic excess for effect or emphasis.[2] For example, when Leti and her friends get thrown out of a San Francisco gay men's bar because it is for gay men only, Leti describes the dive they wind up at as "an old movie-house balcony with seats so sunken-down broken-springs that we might as well have sat on the sticky floor" (104). Then when they find a lively dyke venue, Leti describes the scene as "wall-to-wall delicious dykes and good ambience" (104), a place where she and her lover "messed around in a curtained caboose seat" while being observed by "[t]wo tired corporate-tower types who were totally out of place in the tough vibe of the bar" (104).

The repetitive, tiered descriptions align with the conversational tone of the novel. For example, the narrator engages in many asides, such as claiming that every word of the story is true or asking the reader not to laugh at a particularly salacious or embarrassing detail. After a tangential explanation, the narrator returns to the main narrative thread with a conversational and improvisational-sounding "So anyway . . ." (52) or "I'll be honest . . ." (55). Throughout the book, this becomes not just part of the characters' vernacular but also the descriptive and expressive linguistic style that characterizes the entire narrative. This resonates with the queer black vernacular strategies of Sharon Bridgforth's work, with slashes and renaming creating an expansiveness of description, using expansiveness as a method for approaching specificity or the intensity of emotion: "Our sex wasn't exhibitionism, it was public service of a kind and it made me feel high and mighty and sleepy-eyed just-been-loved" (104). The compound words here serve as stylistic antics and experimentations to do descriptive justice to the playful, hedonistic, and erotic lesbian social scene depicted. At the end of this bar scene Leti's lover K calls her a "Rebel girl" (104), a type of compound in itself that conveys how Leti is not just a rebellious youth but specifically a rebel against the traditional idea of a what a girl should act like.

Lemus also deploys this linguistic play with hyphenated compound verbs that capture action incorporating or falling between two specific verbs. For example, when Leti first meets K, she tries to sound smooth and flirtatious after her best friend embarrasses her by mentioning that she works as a dog groomer. Attempting to recover from the embarrassing career revelation, Leti says, "I kind of laugh-breathed" (64). The compound construction suggests not quite a laugh and not quite a full breath but both simultaneously, suggesting a sense of in-betweenness or too muchness, a sense of not fitting in or of feeling too much discomfort for common language to hold or express.

Lemus resorts to compound or repetitive adjectives to express a single complex idea. She describes a group of boys trying to appear tough as exhibiting "gangster-proud expressions they copied from their older brothers" (77). When describing a lover's mouth, she says that she has "luscious orange lipstick lips" (105), using excessive detail to capture the hyperfeminine seductive excess associated with femme femininity. The flowing adjectives are imitative or expressive of a flowing feminine speech as well as a resourceful inventiveness resonant of the do-it-yourself attitude or aesthetic of the queer punk scene also being depicted. The windy descriptions and tangled phrasings make it sometimes difficult to follow the logic or action or sentence structure, contributing further to the text's "unreadable" sensibility. Lemus's linguistic play amounts to an articulation and creation of a vocabulary that can adequately express genderqueer experience where singular, straightforward wording does not suffice.

In Lemus's first work of queer Chicana fiction, it is clearly the unreadability of genderqueerness, rather than queer desire, that causes a disconnect between the young Chicana protagonist and her Mexican American culture and family.[3] By situating Leti as the central figure in the text, Lemus privileges a working-class genderqueer Chicana dyke subjectivity in a way that few Chicana texts have attempted. These intersecting identity issues have been theorized by Anzaldúa and Moraga, for instance, but they have not for the most part been addressed in very many Chicana novels. What Lemus does with this subjectivity, however, raises a host of questions about how queerness figures into Chicanx identity, particularly in terms of how genderqueer is situated as opposed to or outside the boundaries of Chicanidad.

Leti's grandmother (Nana) becomes a significant player in Leti's identity struggle. Significantly, it is around gender expression—not sexuality—that their relationship becomes threatened. Nana and Leti do not explicitly discuss Leti's sexuality, her dyke identity, or her desire for other women. Throughout the text, Leti has a series of girlfriends but never has a coming-out moment in which she declares her sexuality to Nana, who is her mother figure. This is a curious absence in a lesbian novel but perhaps speaks to the silence that pervades many Chicanx families around issues of sexuality, particularly lesbianism. Leti does not go through a process in which she is wracked with indecision about whether she is a lesbian; she realizes her lesbian identity in college without so much as a second thought. Thus, she does not seem to have an identity crisis over her sexuality, and she does not seem to be faced with any desire to announce her newfound sexual identity to Nana. Whether Nana makes any assumptions about Leti's sexuality is never hinted at in the text, so we can presume that this was either a site of silence or simply a nonissue.

What does become an issue, however, is Leti's gender performance. When Nana visits her on Mother's Day, Leti dons masculine attire for the occasion. She carefully irons one of her "grown-up dress shirts," a "new skinny navy blue tie," and a pair of "new dark brown slacks" (166). This is radically different from how she has dressed before. Although she has occasionally chosen a single marker of masculinity to accent her attire, such as an ex-lover's pair of "Italian zippered boots" (43), she is typically depicted as feminine, wearing short dresses, her favorite pearl choker, and on one occasion a cat suit. Yet, she claims to want to "get dressed proper for Nana" (165) and likens herself to a chemistry "experiment."

Leti also radically alters her hairstyle for the occasion, losing her "sharp-edged bob hairdo," typically coded as feminine, claiming that it "dragged [her] down into a funk and put [her] in tears," despite the fact that we have not been shown any such evidence of her unhappiness with her previous appearance. She opts for a "cropped barbershop clean-cut boy haircut." She changes her appearance in this manner, "hoping that the elements would meld without too harsh an explosion" (165). Thus, she expects some type of "explosion" from Nana's reaction but hopes only that it will not be too harsh.

When the grandmother arrives at Leti's house and sees her dressed in a manly manner, Nana reacts strongly to her gender expression by exclaiming, "Dear Mother of God. Is that a boy or a girl?" (167). Nana's reaction is especially significant because she does not say that Leti looks like a boy or a man; she appears to not understand which sex or gender is being presented. Additionally, Nana does not refer to Leti by name or speak directly to her; she uses the word "that" as though Leti is not a person but an indecipherable object. Thus, Nana makes it clear that it is not Leti's choice to express a masculinity that is a problem. It is the ambiguity of her gender performance that is not readable or tolerated.

In reacting with an appeal to the Virgin Mary ("Mother of God"), Leti's grandmother echoes the language one might use in a Catholic prayer. Opening such an appeal with "Dear" increases the urgency, making the utterance either a direct appeal to the Virgin Mary or an epithet, doubly blasphemous in Chicano Catholic culture because it curses both the holy figure and the sacred figure of the mother. The use of the word "that," because it is a generic pronoun, not a gendered pronoun, emphasizes the volatility associated with upsetting traditional gender categories. Leti, here, is spoken about as an object because she is unidentifiable in terms of specific gender. The generic "that" also distances the two subjects from each other (that over there versus me here). In the absence of a gendered pronoun, the grandmother calls attention to the ubiquitousness of fixed ideas of gender; the grandmother has only the traditional gender binary to understand Leti: that Leti must be either a boy or a girl. The question is also infantilizing; the grandmother does not ask whether Leti is a man or a woman but asks instead whether Leti is a boy or a girl. She also does not speak directly to Leti, instead calling on her higher spiritual power to explain "that" which she sees before her.

While we can interpret the grandmother's reaction as shock, disgust, or dismay at the loss of the possibility of gender normativity, we can also see it simply as a moment of utter confusion. In that moment of her exclamation, the grandmother fails (whether feigning or not) to read Leti because Leti does not register clearly as either female or male. This moment of unreadability according to the traditional gender binary is also a disavowal, a distancing, and ultimately a dehumanizing move that leaves Leti's very personhood in doubt.

That Nana does not ever have such an outburst around Leti's sexuality suggests that silence or denial is the mode of operating around that issue. Leti does not ever specifically come out (here referring to the trope of a discrete declarative event rather than a long-term process) to her grandmother, who serves as Leti's connection to Chicana culture. However, this scene of unreadable gender performance is a type of coming out, one of genderqueerness, and Nana essentially rejects her. Although we may sympathize with Leti's rejection during her coming-out moment, her actions call into question her choice to force the issue in this manner.

After this scene in which the grandmother is shocked by Leti's masculine gender expression, the grandmother suddenly dies. It is as though Leti's gender ambiguity—her unreadability—has killed her Mexican grandmother. Thus, the novel engages in what I call the "killing-the-Mexican syndrome" in which the feminist protagonist can live fully only once the text kills off her Mexican past. Leti also breaks off her relationship with Edith, the other Chicana lesbian in the novel, because she learns that Edith is from an economically privileged background. This severs Leti's only other connection to her Chicanx community.

Leti forms a friendship with a fellow genderqueer working-class white dyke, Nolan. In the novel's final scene, Leti and Nolan, Chicana dyke and white dyke, sit together while Leti waxes nostalgic about stories Nana shared with her of her Mexican heritage. In the end Leti is left with two things: her Chicana stories and her alliance with Nolan. On the one hand, Leti's alliance with Nolan can be seen as transformative because it crosses ethnic borders, even as it leaves the Chicana without her Chicana community. To read this ending, one might be tempted to look to Anzaldúa's borderlands theory to provide a framework for reading the racialized genderqueer Chicana and her predicament around gender, sexuality, class, race, and nation. In *Borderlands/La Frontera*, Anzaldúa argues that the Chicana lesbian has no race or nation (102). And Lemus's novel seems to demonstrate this, in that if Leti wants to be a genderqueer queer person, she can do so only after escaping the boundaries of Chicanx family and community. But in Anzaldúa's vision of the new mestiza, the Chicana lesbian (and Chicana in general) emerges from the crucible that is the borderlands with a transcendent consciousness and a radicalized politic organized around social activism. In Lemus's narrative, the Chicana lesbian is without a nation. She is neither envisioned back into her Chicanx community nor envisioned as altering that nation so it will accept her.

On the one hand, Lemus may seem to imply a forced choice between Chicanx community and queer community for Chicanas who, as Gloria Anzaldúa says, "made the choice to be queer" (*Borderlands/La Frontera* 19). Lemus combines an Anzaldúan facultad, a capacious facility for borderlands metamorphosis, with Moraga's concept of creating a queer Aztlán in which genderqueer Chicanxs reconfigure Chicanidad into their own potentially transformative cultural space.

Lemus's representations of genderqueerness pose questions about what it means to be seen, to be visible, or to be unseen. In *Unexplained Presence*, poet and critic Tisa Bryant extends the work of Toni Morrison's *Playing in the Dark: Whiteness and the Literary Imagination* to explore the unacknowledged black presences in Eurocentric literatures. Bryant troubles the notion of comfort in visibility to gesture toward the power of being unseen. Bryant's work reminds us that for minoritarian subjects, seeking visibility or arriving at a sense of being seen does not necessarily result in power, equity, justice, or positive social change.

Lemus's novel makes genderqueerness visible within a Chicanx frame yet seems to remain uncomfortable with "mere" visibility. Lemus's text provokes an exploration of how and why queers figure as unreadable to other Chicanxs in the worlds imagined by contemporary Chicana literature. It causes us to ask how moments of unreadability of the other may be interpreted not as a disavowal but instead as an opportunity for self-construction, how this can be not just a loss or a rendering invisible but also a productive, generative moment that in fact constitutes a self, a subject in question. As Stryker et al. point out, "Transing can function as a disciplinary tool when the stigma associated with the lack or loss of gender status threatens social unintelligibility, coercive normalization, or even bodily extermination. It can also function as an escape vector, line of flight, or pathway toward liberation" (13). In *Trace Elements of Random Tea Parties,* this escape vector seems to move away from Chicanx community.

Lemus's second novel, *Like Son,* however, further explores gender variant subjectivities in relation to Chicanidad. Transing in *Like Son* connects present-day transgender Chicanx bodies to a lost Chicanx past. Whereas Mexico as homeland has served this function in constructing ideas of Chicanidad in previous Chicanx literature, crossing in the body in *Like Son* allows for the crossing of time and place, making the trans body a site of possibilities for broadening definitions of Chicanidad.

The novel features a female-to-male (FTM) transgender protagonist named Frank Cruz, who struggles with coming to terms with his father's death and the haunting of untold family histories. The narrative unravels a hidden family history, centering around the avant-garde artist and writer Nahui Olin's courting of Frank's grandmother and particularly a moment in which the two women (Nahui and the grandmother) kiss publicly at a fountain in the center of the town plaza in Mexico City, causing a family scandal in the 1920s. As it becomes revealed that the untold family histories center around deviant sexualities, Frank discovers that he is not the first in his family to turn away from heteronormativity and gender conformity. The history of gender nonconformity and queerness in the family has been passed down the generations via a cryptic archive of hidden photographs and inscriptions in a book.

The unspeakable presence and history of queerness within Frank's Mexican American family becomes for him a source of intrigue and inspiration. His desire to uncover his family's hidden legacy of desire drives him to abandon his current life in search of his family's past. He begins hearing or imagining the voices of ancestors, including the voice of Nahui Olin, whose picture he carries in his wallet. As Catrióna Rueda Esquibel discusses in *With Her Machete in Her Hand,* this search for a queer familial history is a recurring theme in Chicana lesbian literature, and this is also the case in this transgender novel. Additionally, many Chicana lesbian-authored texts, according to Esquibel, bear some direct relationship to the Chicano movement, or at least to mainstreamed collective Chicanx history. Lemus's search for queer Chicanx history focuses on an individual, not collective, search. Lemus complicates this theme by taking up transgender experiences and issues, albeit without necessarily drawing on the language of contemporary mainstream white queer culture.

The story shifts locales between Los Angeles, New York City, and Mexico City; the novel shifts the locus of queer Chicanx experience away from the West Coast and the Southwest to New York. The story incorporates the events of 9/11, and although the characters are not directly involved, they are impacted by haunting nightmares that suggest connections between a traumatic historical event and the daily emotional trauma of being a transgender person in a transphobic world. Although the narrative centers around a transgender character, it does not explain much about Frank's transition. In *With Her Machete in Her Hand* the story begins when Frank is "a man of thirty" (9), and there is little explanation of how or why he made his transition other than deciding that he feels more natural as a boy and begins wearing baggy "skater clothes." This lack of explanation leaves a cloud of mystery around Frank; on the other hand, it normalizes trans experience and also resistance to living only within a traditional gender binary.[4] The focus is not on Frank's transition but rather on how his sense of his own gender variance is constructed in relation to his Mexican American family of origin as he separates from them into a queer adulthood.

As Lemus's second novel to engage questions of Chicanx gender variance, *Like Son* is an extension of the thematics explored in *Trace Elements of Random Tea Parties,* particularly gender variance and how it impacts and is impacted by familia, homeland, and loss. Early in the narrative, Frank's ailing, blind father dies. His death becomes a rite of passage in which Frank inherits the trappings of his father's Mexican American masculinity. Immediately after his father dies, Frank hears his father's voice telling him to keep his suits. Frank's father never saw him wearing a suit, nor do they discuss his dress. Indeed, while his father is alive, he does not acknowledge or express awareness of Frank's identification as a transgender man. He insists on calling Frank by the childhood nicknames Paquita or "Francisca, baby girl" (*Like Son* 16), to which Frank has an uncomfortable visceral response, although he does not speak up. Frank's preference for silence about being a trans man is highlighted in a scene in which Frank and his formerly estranged father are sharing a meal in a diner. Frank's internal monologue focuses on his experience of gender as a child and a teen. He reflects on his father's lack of knowledge of this aspect of Frank's life (18). As Frank contemplates this, the waitress approaches to take their order and addresses Frank with the question "Son?" Frank's elderly father, who is blind, thinks this is a flattering or flirtatious remark directed at him and responds.[5] Franks says nothing about this to his father but notes the moment: "He was totally clueless. But still, I'd passed in front of my father" (19). Uncertain how his father may react to learning that Frank is trans, Frank opts to keep silent, maintaining a degree of privacy from his family member.

Frank reflects that as a child, he wondered why his father always wore dressy clothes rather than the casual jeans and T-shirts worn by the other kids' fathers. In response to being asked about this habit of dress, the father responds by saying "Don't ever let anyone call you a lazy wetback" (15). Frank reflects on this response and tries to draw connections to his own experience:

> I had no idea how that was an answer to my question. I tried asking my magic fish, but upon closer inspection, its envelope claimed it could tell me only if I was in love, lucky, or tired. Fifteen years later, I'd been dealt enough jabs—including one incident in junior high when a group of kids threw handfuls of pennies at me, called me a "beaner queer whore," and were only reprimanded by the lunch supervisor to *Sit down and eat*—that I'd come to understand my father's reasons for wanting to present a polished front. His attire and grooming was passive resistance of a most dignified form. (16)

The polished front donned by the father is a form of resistance against the daily "jabs" of racism. The construction "beaner queer whore" conflates the racial epithet "beaner" with nonnormative sexuality ("queer") and sexual promiscuity ("whore"). The passage speaks to the intertwining of race, sexuality, and gender expression. That this slur is lobbed at the protagonist along with "handfuls of pennies" associates such a construction with economic poverty as well. The throwing of the pennies at the Mexican American child evokes the stereotype of poor Mexican children in need of a handout as well as the collective anxiety that erupts in the United States around providing public welfare to the poor, particularly newly arrived immigrants.[6] Frank's realization about belonging and the importance of keeping up appearances creates a connection between race and queerness.

A few of the objects that Frank's father bequeaths to him include a photograph of Nahui Ohlin, a beautiful Mexican woman whose identity is at first unclear to Frank. Frank carries around her picture, given to him by his father for safekeeping. Besides the photograph, there is also a book containing Nahui's poetry. Through the poetry Frank learns the significance of Nahui Ohlin's name, which refers to the "fifth sun," or the current age, according to ancient Mexica cosmology. Although Nahui Ohlin is based on an actual historical figure of the 1920s avant-garde muralista movement, typically associated with the likes of Frida Kahlo and Diego Rivera, not much is known about her life. Thus, Nahui provides a site upon which to frame a fictionalized, imagined queer Mexican history. Frank's girlfriend Natalie, whom he first meets in New York, becomes the vehicle for uncovering the mysteries of Nahui Ohlin. Natalie also becomes a site of embodiment of Nahui, taking on her mannerisms and dress and becoming a site on which Frank can project and enact his fantasies of who Nahui is to him. As Frank imagines himself Nahui's lover, he enacts what his grandmother could not do in her day, which is to express desire for a woman.

Against the inheritance from the father figure, disavowal, or the threat of disavowal, the mother figure looms prominently in both of Lemus's novels. In *Trace Elements of Random Tea Parties,* although the grandmother does not necessarily reject Leti, she does react with shock to Leti's masculine gender expression and dies soon thereafter. In *Like Son,* Frank is rejected by his traditional Chicana mother—again, not because of sexuality but because he has chosen to live as a man. When the novel begins, Frank is estranged from his mother and has not seen her in over five years. When his father dies, Frank visits his mother to let her know about the death. When Frank arrives at his mother's house, his mother seems or claims not to recognize him, speaking to him through the locked screen door: "'Who are you?' she had the nerve to ask" (69). Frank dismisses his mother's reaction as her "vintage insane behavior," and he contemplates his own interior answers to the question: "I was the child she probably wished she'd never had. I was a person who wanted out of the life I was born into. But there was one thing I most definitely wasn't . . . I was *not* my mother's daughter" (69). Frank calls attention to the fact that he is not the child his mother might have imagined for herself.

In fact, Frank has become his father's son. When he shows up on his mother's doorstep, with a wooden box of his father's ashes in his hand, it becomes clear that the version of masculinity Frank has inherited is a working-class Mexican masculinity. While waiting at his mother's front door, he reminisces about his mother's disapproval of him when he was presenting as a tomboyish adolescent girl. Frank recalls to himself that "[a]ll I knew was that I was a boy and that being a boy felt safe and true and right" (69). This is one of the only moments in the text in which Frank mentions his feelings about being male. It is precisely in this revelatory moment when his mother's rejection is most harshly pronounced that she looks at him pointedly and expresses her shame: "'Do you realize what people say about you?' Her eyes scanned me up and down" (71). His mother proceeds to hand him a stash of money even though he says he does not want the money. When she closes the door in his face, Frank imagines himself a horned devil standing at her door:

> She didn't want any neighbors who might be looking down from
> their own hilly views to catch sight of her slamming the door
> on the miserable horned creature standing on her *Welcome* mat.
> Horns. Yes, I'm certain I had horns emerging from my temples.
> My father did too. (72)

Frank's vision of himself as a monstrous devil emphasizes how his mother sees him as no longer readable as her daughter yet not fully legible as a "real" man. Though he sees himself as a man and presents as man, his raced and classed masculinity seems insufficient. As Jack Halberstam notes, "Masculinity . . . becomes legible as masculinity where and when it leaves the white male middle-class body. . . . Arguments about excessive masculinity tend to focus on black bodies (male and female), Latino/a bodies, or working-class bodies, and insufficient masculinity" (*Female Masculinity* 2).

Although Frank momentarily sees himself as a devil, like his father, and struggles with what that might mean, he reveals his anger toward his mother:

> She said, "You have your father's blood in you," and I saw in
> her eyes all the times my father had grabbed her tiny wrists and
> forced her to listen, the times he had screamed and thrown things

against walls. I was not violent, but, unforgivable as it was, I did understand why my father had snapped with anger at her. (72)

The mother's declaration that Frank is just like his father evokes the title of the novel, *Like Son*, which suggests the saying "Like father, like son," an expression that attributes a son's characteristics and behaviors as typical or mimetic of his father's. The title also suggests that the protagonist is "like" a son, an approximation or a failed attempt but not quite considered an actual or real son. Also, the title could also be read as an invitation or command to sympathize with the son character, particularly in the scene in which his mother rejects him. Frank's anger toward his mother in this scene amounts to a refusal of her rejection of his working-class Mexican masculinity. Given the pressure toward upward class mobility in his family and his mother's disdain, the trans masculinity that Frank takes on is a racialized, classed masculinity, complicating his struggle at attempting to rewrite what his Mexican American masculinity can mean.

Before Frank returns to New York from his trip to his mother's house in Los Angeles, he returns his father's artifacts to a safety deposit box in L.A. These items include Nahui's artifacts and a few of his father's last effects, handed down from Frank's Mexican grandmother, who migrated from Mexico to the United States. Frank's returning the items to the safety deposit box could be read simply as a cutting off, a disowning or putting away of his Mexicanness, his family's collective memory. Or perhaps his actions suggest a moving on, the progression of grief toward a healthy acceptance. As Frank turns away from dwelling on loss toward letting it go, perhaps his queer family history is not needed. The artifacts are not destroyed, but neither are they carried around and displayed in his home any longer, indicating that a proper mourning has run its course. Perhaps this is like putting away an altar, which is typically perpetually displayed and cared for in a traditional Mexican American home. The grief for an unknown or unclear family past is no longer needed after it has been worked through. Because he travels from New York back to L.A. to return the items and decides to root himself in New York, even symbolically planting a tree in the middle of a New York street, the narrative may suggest a putting away of Chicanx dreams of reclaiming the symbolic site of the mythical homeland of Aztlán and moving eastward toward modern urban life where genderqueerness can flourish.[7] In the end, Frank's moving on from Nahui Ohlin, the "fifth sun," may be his way of moving on to a newer world, severing himself from his Mexican@ and Chicanx past.

If the figure of La Malinche, Cortés's translator and mistress, has provided a way for Chicanx feminists to refigure themselves as cultural translators and strategic traitors of their race, then Lemus's post-borderlands narratives suggest that the figure of Coyolxauh-qui offers an apt analogy for the experiences of Chicanx gender variant people in Lemus's work. Coyolxauhqui, although typically described as female, is actually dually sexed and represents both male and female powers. She is killed by her warrior brother for attempting to usurp their mother's power. After he dismembers her he throws her body parts up into the sky, and she becomes the moon.[8] The reassembled and reconstructed body of Coyolxauhqui is reconstituted and reimagined beyond the gender binary as the quintessential post-borderlands subject.[9]

Lemus's texts make interventions within Chicanx literature as well as within racialized constructions of gender and sexuality. By exploring how genderqueerness and transgender experiences are in question within Chicanx familial and cultural contexts, we can understand how loss, absence, rejection, and ejections become productive sites of struggle and meaning making for the Chicanx genderqueer and transgender subjects. Lemus's novels illuminate the idea expressed by transgender activist Leslie Feinberg in *Trans Liberation,* which is that "[m]any of us have identities we have no language for" (69). While this might be a common sentiment for people who do not experience themselves as fitting into normative categories of belonging or identity, it resonates strongly with the queer Chicanx subjects of Lemus's novels.

In a 2007 interview on the literary blog *Bookslut,* author Lemus remarks that "I really, truly just wanted to write a story where I have a protagonist that can be transgendered, like Frank is, where it wouldn't be about his transgenderism, where it would be about his life" (Zuarino n.p.). In response to the interviewer's claim that "[i]t seems like every time someone writes an LGBTQ character, it's about their *sexuality* or their *coming-out* or their *sex*," Lemus responds "Yeah, very often. I'm not so much interested in trying to normalize it or make it invisible. Someone paid me a huge compliment and said that, in their opinion, *Like Son* is a *post-trans* novel. In a way, it's like a *post-queer* novel where, of course, it's a central part of the book, but it's moved further out."

At times Felicia Luna Lemus's fiction seems to move the Chicanx queer out of Chicanx community, aligning somewhat with the borderlands literary legacy of Chicana lesbian authors Anzaldúa and Moraga. Yet Lemus's work also signals a productive move, a move toward a post-borderlands, in which gender variance and queerness of gender—and not just queerness of sexuality—must be taken into account. Lemus's contemporary portrayals of queerness and her transing of Chicanidad move us toward a greater understanding of the intersectionalities of race, ethnicity, class, sexuality, gender, and gender identities through the productive unreadability of transgressive, racialized Chicanx genders.

4

Brokeback Rancho

To begin to theorize gender and sexuality as distinct though intimately entangled axes of analysis has been, indeed, a great advance of recent lesbian and gay thought.... There is danger, however, that that advance may leave the effeminate boy once more in the position of the haunting abject—this time the haunting abject of gay thought itself.
—Eve Sedgwick, *Tendencies*

Luis Gonzaga and Carl Devlin prayed that they might go East together in summer.
—Jovita González and Eve Raleigh, *Caballero*

Nearly one hundred years after the Treaty of Guadalupe Hidalgo marked the official end of the U.S.-Mexico War and forged a significant portion of Mexico into the U.S. Southwest, a folklorist and historian named Jovita González set out to chronicle what she saw as the loss of a distinctly Mexican way of life along the U.S.-Mexican border. While Margaret Mitchell's 1936 *Gone with the Wind* attempted to romanticize the story of the American Civil War in the American imagination, William Faulkner's novels complicated the idea of whiteness in the antebellum U.S. South, and Richard Wright's 1938 *Uncle Tom's Children* confronted readers with the harsh social realism of black survival in Jim Crow America, Jovita González's fiction ambitiously sought to put Mexican America on the map.

González's historical novel *Caballero* fictionalizes the 1848 moment and the impact that this crucial turning point had on the predominantly rural and ranch-dependent populations of what is now South Texas, where ranch owners and workers suddenly found themselves to be the first inhabitants of a newly colonized Mexican America. The novel's narrative thrust follows members of the Mendoza y Soría family upon the U.S. Anglo invasion of Mexico and the resultant tumultuous transition in which much of the Mexican owning class was catapulted into the hordes of dispossessed in a newly recolonized territory.

Among the cast of displaced characters in Jovita González's account of the early Mexican American borderlands appears Luis Gonzaga. Luis is an effeminate and artistic gentleman. His own father describes him as a marica (faggot) unfit to inherit the vast landholdings of Rancho La Palma de Cristo. This queerly gendered figure emerges in a seemingly unlikely source, a 1930s historical novel in which the Mexican ranchero Luis Gonzaga falls in love with the Anglo U.S. military officer Captain Carl Devlin. Sixty years before the *New Yorker* published Annie Proulx's gay cowboy love story "Brokeback Mountain," Mexican American author Jovita González was exploring gay cowboy love in the historical romance that eventually became the novel *Caballero*.[1] Why would a historical fiction of ethnic Mexicans in the United States, written in a time and place historically—and contemporaneously—fraught with divisive racial tensions, concern itself with the marica, the Mexican American queer? And how does González's *Caballero* figure into the narrative of Mexican American and American literature? These are some of the critical questions I explore as I consider the queer content as well as the queer context of the novel's writing, loss, rediscovery, and production.

Although *Caballero* was written in the 1930s, the novel was rejected by publishers during González's lifetime and was not published until it was discovered in her archives by José Limón and María Cotera in the 1990s. Published in 1996, *Caballero* prompted reconsiderations of pre–World War II Mexican American literary production.[2] Additionally, González's proper place in the narrative of Mexican American literature continues to be plagued by uncertainties about her possible coauthor, Margaret Eimer, who used the pen name Eve Raleigh and whose exact role in coauthoring the novel remains open to question.

Limón and Cotera's laudable recovery of González's novel certainly marked a significant textual event in Chicanx studies. Their recovery of González's lost manuscripts also opens avenues of possibility. Building on their work, I would like to take up questions of queerness and gender variance within and around González's work. The novel's significant focus on the queer character of Luis Gonzaga has gone mostly unremarked in the book's critical reception, considered alongside what I consider to be queer gaps in the story of González's authorial collaboration, and this allows for an exciting opportunity to contribute further to the recovery project. The case of Jovita González allows us to draw connections between heritage recovery projects and queer recovery projects, particularly when the texts and textures recovered from those archives intersect. González's resurfaced *Caballero* prompts us to examine what it means to include González's work in a queer Chicanx cultural and literary lineage.

I am arguing for the integral role of genderqueerness or nonnormative gender expression in redefining Mexican American cultural imaginaries, and in this chapter I question what it means to construct knowledge of queer borderlands experience through a recovered text. I examine the politics of the recovery and critical reception of González's *Caballero*, and I discuss how we might make use of González's novel as a case for reconsidering the interdisciplinary issues and implications of queer readings of recovered minoritarian texts more broadly. In interrogating the relationships between Chicana literary production and knowledge production, I argue for a rethinking of González's work as a contribution not just to a Chicana literary archive but also to a *queer* Chicana literary archive.

Critics have tended to regard Jovita González's novel *Caballero* as somewhat critical but largely celebratory of the union between Anglo and Mexican cultures in the context of the violent circumstances by which such contact came about (Limón, Cotera, J. González).

I would add, however, that the novel also provides an alternative affective history of the borderlands as well as an alternative queer historical fiction. A predominant theme that courses through the narrative is the patriarch's fear of domination, particularly through the effeminization of masculinist Mexican culture, and his ultimate resignation and utter hopelessness that his sense of Mexicanness will survive the U.S. Anglo conquest of northern Mexico.

I contend that it is not just race or class or gender or sexuality but rather genderqueerness that provides a mechanism through which González constructs an alternative affective, queer history of the Mexican American borderlands that explores the fear of colonial domination, particularly through the effeminization of culture and the expressions of nonheteronormative sexualities and genders. *Caballero* also queers the historical romance genre, complicating ideas about the relationship and "marriage" of two nations.[3] Further, *Caballero* can also be said to explore a liminal space and time between colonial and postcolonial moments and subjectivities. The novel's queer content is unusual for an early or premovimiento Mexican American work of fiction (the novel was written in the 1930s and is set in the mid-nineteenth century). It was not until the publication of John Rechy's work in the 1960s and 1970s that gay male Chicano sexuality was openly discussed in literary works, making González's willingness to represent queer Mexicanidad worthy of attention. Additionally, the novel's gender-queer intervention marks it as particularly unusual and untimely for an early twentieth-century novel. Given the historical erasures and recovery project, it seems productive to at least open this line of questioning around the impact of authorial anxiety and attendant questions of "authenticity" and their impact on or relationship to the queer content and context of the book.

My goal here in a queer reading of *Caballero* is threefold. First, I want to recover a queer artifact of Mexican American literary culture and articulate the implications of such a recovery. Second, in claiming González as a contributor to a queer Mexican American archive, I demonstrate how her fiction prefigured some of the Chicana lesbian feminist concerns expressed in literary texts of the late twentieth century. Third, throughout this process of queer re-recovery, I uncover the unlikely and integral role that queerness plays in the construction of Mexican American cultural imaginaries.

To give an example of how *Caballero* invites us to think queerly about gender in the early U.S.-Mexican borderlands, I would like to highlight a key passage from the text in which Luis Gonzaga and Captain Devlin see each other for the first time. The scene reads like a typical moment of love at first sight, with both men immediately captivated by the other. As Luis and his brother Alvaro and their vaqueros ride across a stream on their father's vast ranch, they unexpectedly encounter a group of mounted U.S. military officers crossing the stream in the opposite direction. Struck by the sight of the U.S. captain, Luis stops to stare. Equally struck, Captain Devlin stares back at Luis. The full passage reads as follows:

> The last one [Luis] stayed on the bank, sheer curiosity in the searching look he gave the Americans. Devlin slowed to return it in kind, smiled, and stopped. He reminded him of one of El Greco's portraits. Surely this lad was no rancher. He looked like a poet or an artist should look—and so seldom did. And on the striking black-maned dun pony, sitting on the elaborately trimmed saddle with the ease of a long familiarity with it, he made a picture which thrilled Devlin through and through. He was about to speak to him when an insolent voice called, "Come on, Luis Gonzaga, can't you find anything better to look at than a gringo's face?"
>
> A blush suffused the sensitive face as he answered, "I'm coming, Alvaro." He gave Devlin a last glance after he turned, then spurred the dun into the water.
>
> Later in the evening, when warming themselves by the fire . . . , Devlin remarked casually, "I hope I meet that boy under more pleasant circumstances. I like him. Rather more than merely like him." (48)

Through a contemporary queer lens, it is impossible not to be struck by the audacity of the characters openly expressing their desire for each other as well as González's boldness in interweaving this homoerotic story into this historical novel.[4] When Alvaro chastises Luis for giving his attention to a "gringo's face," his rebuke frames the rigid expectations of the gendered as well as cross-racial behavior demanded of Luis. With multiple taboos mobilized at once, the two men, one a Mexican rancher and the other an Anglo soldier tasked with seizing control of the land and its people for U.S. control, enter into a dangerous cross-cultural, same-sex connection.

This passage of the Mexican and Anglo men meeting along the water recalls the moment of contact between the Mexica indigenous peoples and Spanish colonizing forces. Like the legend of the Mexica assuming that the conquistadors on horseback were gods arriving according to prophecy, Luis is struck by the vision of the white army officer approaching on horseback. Indeed, in the 1840s in which this novel begins, whiteness would still be considered an unusual and spectacular sight to the local brown people in northern Mexico.[5]

The men on horseback fulfill, at least visually, the picture of the gentlemen, the idealized masculine American cowboy and vaquero figures of the U.S. Southwest. To Devlin, Luis looks like a poet— like a poet seldom does, evoking an idyllic image of what a gentleman poet should look like and also suggesting that poets do not usually look like a Mexican. What's a poet doing riding a horse on a ranch in Mexico? The use of the colloquial "gringo" rather than the proper "Americano" within earshot of the American soldiers suggests both the language differences and the intense emotions at work. Alvaro's use of the derogatory term "gringo" captures the anger and tension of the Mexican ranchers under invasion. When Luis's older brother Alvaro chastises Luis in front of the Americans, he demonstrates his superior status as older brother of the ranchland. Yet Alvaro's anger seems directed at Luis's fascination with the gringo, at how intensely both men are struck by the sight of each other, and at the openness of their intimate visual exchange. At issue is how Luis is struck by men, by their faces, not by socially acceptable objects of desire such as Mexican women and their bodies.

Caballero situates South Tejas as the locus of international and ideological warfare between the U.S. Anglo imperial project and the network of microempires that constituted the Mexican hacienda ranching system, which operated in relative autonomy given their far-flung geographic distance from the central seat of Mexican national government, which had only been independent from Spain since 1821 and relied heavily on the localized sufficiency of the paternalistic agrarian system. In González's fictional account of Mexico's failed defense against the United States, it is not just Anglo dominance but also Mexican patriarchy and hacienda provincialism against which many Mexicans resist. Within the narrative's historical frame constructed and reimagined by González, the novel disrupts binaries of south/north, Mexican/Anglo, colonized/colonizer, and ally/enemy. It also complicates what a gendered critique of Mexican and American/Anglo patriarchy entails in that it raises questions not just of female/male experience or queer/straight sexualities but also of nonnormative/normative gender expressions—in this case via the effeminate marica.

Significantly, the character of Luis is established not just as queer but also as an artist. The local priest (Padre Pierre) notices Luis's artistic inclination and provides him with art supplies so he can paint portraits of the saints, but the portraits he creates are too worldly and "unsaintlike" (such as Saint Cecilia at the harp). When the priest learns that Devlin is interested in art as well, he shows Devlin some of Luis's sketches. Devlin learns from the priest that Luis is an outcast and that his father calls him marica, and he asks the priest to arrange a meeting with Luis (105). The men meet in the church, and Devlin says that he wants "to possess the liveliness of Luis's art." He tells Luis that if he is serious about his art, then he should be practicing/studying art in Baltimore, which thrills Luis (106). Devlin and the priest seem privy to knowledge they desire to share with Luis: "Shall I tell our friend of us and our land?" asks Devlin, to which the priest replies "Do." (106). This conversation reads as coded language for some secret joto-landia or gay utopia. Luis returns home after his meeting with Devlin and the priest, and Luis's father expresses disapproval at his son's art supplies (108).

Soon after, Luis sees Devlin at the Catholic church in town. Luis wants desperately to touch Devlin's hand. Luis puts his hand on Devlin's hands, and the two men stand holding each other's hands for a few minutes while talking. Luis is so distracted by Devlin that he forgets he is supposed to monitor his sister's behavior and fails to see that Robert Warrener has been holding Susanita's hand, breaking a social code that prohibits touching the hand of an unmarried woman without parental or familial supervision (117). When Luis and his sister Susanita discuss her love for the Anglo soldier Robert Warrener, they make a sibling pact and agree to keep the shared secret. Luis does not reveal his desire to go to Baltimore with Devlin (108), but we do learn through narrative description that "Luis Gonzaga and Carl Devlin prayed that they might go East together in summer" (118).

Beyond the queer content of the novel itself, the queer story of the book's production history gives rise to a queer feeling about Jovita and her work. It raises questions about what it means to press the author's life or presumed identity into service when examining how queerness is constructed and represented in the novel. In the introduction to *Caballero*, Limón details what is known of the collaboration between the novel's coauthors, Jovita González and Eve Raleigh, real name Margaret Eimer (xviii). Based on extensive archival analysis, Limón deduces that González's collaborator may have influenced the formulation of González's original fictionalized ethnographic narrative into a romance novel, although as Limón notes "the historical data and events and, perhaps more importantly, the development of the novel's characters were largely González's contribution to the project" (xxi). That Limón "strongly believe[s] that Eimer had a strong authorial hand in shaping the romantic plot development of *Caballero*" (xxi) suggests that the marriage of the U.S. South and Greater Mexico depicted in *Caballero* is partly a U.S. southern construction, not just a Mexican construction. As Limón notes, not much is known about Eimer's origins, but it is known that she and González probably met in Del Rio, Texas, and that the two women continued collaborating and corresponding after González moved with her husband to

San Antonio and after Eimer, who did not marry, moved with her uncle to Missouri.

In *Native Speakers*, Cotera argues for "gendering the politics of collaboration in *Caballero*" (203) and acknowledging the "erotic collaboration" (223) between the fictional artists Luis and Devlin and its resonances with the authors' collaboration. Cotera says that "Luis's determination to pursue a life of creativity, and to do so alongside his 'enemy' Captain Devlin, thematizes the transformative collaborative desire at the heart of coauthored novels like *Caballero*" (223). Cotera notes that "the text's 'collaborators'—both Anglo and Mexican—transgress the boundaries of race, nation, custom, and heteronormativity to form more perfect unions with former enemies" (218).[6] Cotera goes so far as to ask "[m]ight these collaborations and romantic liaisons reflect the material conditions of *Caballero's* production, the myriad negotiations in the process of writing a collaborative text?" (203). Yet, we can further consider the erotics of collaboration between González and Eimer as a queer endeavor. In "The First Last Generation," Lee Bebout says that "despite the interethnic antagonisms and hostilities that marked the South Texas of the early twentieth century, *Caballero* and the authorial relationship that produced it suggest something queer indeed, that relations and desires may transgress immediate social tensions and not rely on heterosexual reproduction" (370). Because her life has all the traditional trappings and markers of heterosexual coupledom, González is illegible or unreadable as queer. Eimer remained unmarried throughout her life. But González's depiction of Luis as the queer artist who must collaborate with Anglo culture provides a key for reading the queer collaborations and couplings that fill and surround the narrative. The gendered collaboration certainly cannot be cordoned off from the racial collaboration of González and Eimer's crossing of racial boundaries in their Mexican-Anglo collaborative effort. Indeed, their collaboration may also be read as a same-sex collaboration, a labor of love between women.

As Cotera elsewhere notes, "There is a kind of dominant narrative about Jovita González's interactions with the founding fathers of Texas history and folklore studies. The narrative goes something like this: Jovita González, daughter of the old (*Tejano*) order, collaborated with the sons of the new (Anglo) order, but did so with a degree of ambivalence that complicates the generally nostalgic tone of her folklore work" ("Introduction: A Woman of the Borderlands" 4). Cotera further explains that "[s]cholarly assessments of González's folklore writing have generally gravitated between readings of her ideology as either 'accommodationist' or, in the best case, as engaging in a form of muted resistance. The tenor and narrative structure of this [*Landmark*], her earliest lengthy analysis of the border and its people suggests a much more oppositional and resistant subject" (29). According to Cotera, "For González the 'founding fathers' of Texas were not the heroes of the Texas Revolution—Austin, Bowie, Houston—but the Criollo and Mestizo heads of families who established ranches along the Rio Grande in the eighteenth century. Her recovery of the story of their settlement of South Texas establishes the rootedness of Mexicans in Texas and thus counteracts the 'rhetoric of dominance' [Garza-Falcón] that sought to make them invisible" (17). Cotera rightfully claims that "in González's version of Texas history the Texas Revolution and the U.S.-Mexico War fade into relative obscurity, and become simply two more examples in a long history of 'border troubles' whose origins were essentially transnational in nature" (18). González's attentiveness to daily life, women's experience, and queer experience certainly takes center stage as she seeks to bring these invisible histories to the fore.

Limón and Cotera's textual recovery of González's *Caballero* did more than merely add an entry to the revised canon of Mexican American literary products; it was a major textual event that invited scholars in multiple fields to reimagine literary and historical narratives of American histories of the U.S. conquest of Mexico. With limited information and partial manuscripts at hand, the editors pieced together two separate versions of the novel, selecting from each manuscript to build the published edition. In the process, they established Jovita González as the primary author. González's recovered *Caballero* novel is one of the few documents, literary or historical, to relate ethnographic accounts from early

Mexican Texas. Limón and Cotera speculate that González wrote the novel in the 1930s, based largely on her research of folklore and family histories from the generations of Mexicans who experienced what was commonly called "the invasion of the Americanos." Given the evidentiary gaps in the record of early literary efforts by Mexicans in the United States, the publication of such a book indeed carries great cultural significance.

Discovery of the manuscript of *Caballero* was facilitated by a 1970s interview of the author conducted by historian Martha Cotera, María Cotera's mother. The elder Cotera verified the existence of the unfound novel when interviewing Jovita González and her husband E. E. Mireles. During the course of this interview, Mr. Mireles claimed to have destroyed the manuscript of *Caballero* to protect his wife from political backlash against Mexicans in South Texas. However, Jovita González slyly indicated otherwise, wagging her finger in a gesture of "No" that only the interviewer could see. Unbeknownst to her husband, Jovita González signaled to Cotera that the manuscript still existed. This revelation enabled Martha Cotera to report her findings to María Cotera and José Limón, who finally located the manuscript in an archival repository in South Texas. Once the scholars discovered the manuscript, they edited and published it as the novel *Caballero*, thereby placing Jovita González among the handful of the first Mexican American women authors of the twentieth century. Significantly, González remains among the few known Mexican American authors prior to the Chicano movement of the 1960s and 1970s.

González's manuscripts were typed on the reverse side of recycled sheets—discarded pages from manuscripts, personal correspondence, and so forth. Presumably, unused sheets of the finest quality available to the authors would be preferred for presenting their "final" manuscript to New York publishing houses. We can surmise from the coauthors' correspondence and from their "Authors' Notes" (marked as the "Foreword" in the typescript) that they considered the copy (found by Limón) to be an "uncorrected" carbon copy. It is this uncorrected version that the editors compiled, along with chapters from the other manuscript, into the finalized novel.

In fixing the text of *Caballero*, the editors attempted to resolve the question of authorial collaboration in order to restore Jovita González to primary authorship. The title page of the first published edition of *Caballero* (1996) contrasted against a copy of the original title page from the original manuscript reveals how the question of authorship remains open to interpretation. The title page of the original typescript listed a coauthor, Eve Raleigh, identified as a pseudonym for Margaret Eimer, an unknown figure whose authorial—and authoritative—role remains questionable. (Note the significance of Eimer's choice to discard her German surname in favor of the pseudonym Raleigh, evoking a southern gentility designed, without a doubt, to position the novel as a U.S. southern Anglo epic rather than merely a southwestern Mexican American story.) According to the typed manuscript, the centered title reads as follows: "CABALLERO / An historical novel by / Eve Raleigh / and / Jovita Gonzalez" [*sic*]. The original title page lists two authors. The prominent placement of Eve Raleigh's name and mailing address on the top left positions her as the one who has "submitted" the manuscript, presumably to the three publishers discussed in their various correspondence. Notably, in one letter from Eimer to González, Eimer apologies for placing her name first but claims that she did so because a potential publisher she was in communication with had assumed that she was merely "the compiler."

The coeditors sought to locate evidence of the "real" person behind the figure of the pseudonym, attempting to determine her role in authoring—and authorizing—the manuscript. They were unable to do so, raising questions about Raleigh as an unverifiable coauthor or possible ghost author. The editors were also unable to disprove Raleigh's contributions. Thus, they included her name on the title page. However, the editors reversed the order of the names as they appeared in the only existing title page in the manuscripts, placing González above Raleigh.

In piecing together the textual puzzle, the editors filled in what they refer to as narrative gaps, attempting to avoid disrupting the narrative flow. In the manuscripts, the authors marked some long passages "omit" or removed them from one version of the manuscript. The editors included some of these omitted passages into the final text, asserting that their omission would disturb the coherence of the story. For example, one authorial deletion subsequently overridden by the editors removes the narrative possibility of heavenly intervention to protect Mexico from U.S. domination. In one passage in the manuscripts, González (or perhaps Eimer acting as coauthor or preliminary editor) made handwritten corrections to delete a section in which the Mexican protagonist, a Catholic and a landowning gentleman, imagines the Virgin Mary watching over his ranchlands prior to the American invasion: "He would not have been surprised, so carried away was he for the moment, if the Virgin herself in her robe of blue had come floating over the gateway, hands stretched out to them, praying with them." This authorial revision may reveal the conflicting desires of the author. González frequently drew on her ethnographic research, in which she documented Catholic and folk spiritual ritual practices in South Texas, in order to create folkloric representations of the Mexican experience. However, marking these passages for omission suggests that González was in the process of revising her novel into a more palatable narrative, compromising or altering wording in order to avoid accusations of pro-Catholic, pro-Mexican (i.e., anti-American) sentiment. Despite her deletion of this passage, the editors chose to include it in the published version.

At the word and sentence level, some items not legible to the editors remain so marked in the printed edition. For example, in the first chapter, a Mexican woman expresses disgust at the suggestion that Mexicans in what has become the U.S. Southwest must choose whether to become citizens of the United States. She exclaims, "We do not choose to be [dirty] *Americanos*" (9). In the noted explanation, the editors explain as follows: "Bracketed word is marked out by a single line in MS2. We restore it here for the evident ideological import of this change" (347, note 6).

While the authors' queer love story, no doubt questionable for its time, remains prominently included throughout both of their original manuscripts, my own comparison of the manuscripts revealed one intriguing sentence marked for omission by the authors that was also omitted by the editors. In an earlier version of the *Caballero* manuscript, a passage in which Luis and his sister Susana discuss secrets pushes at the edges of allowable nonheteronormativity. In what purports to be the earlier draft of the manuscript, there is a sentence that speaks volumes about how González, and perhaps her coauthor, may have imagined Luis and Devlin's narrative of same-sex desire as analogous to the romance plot between Susana and Warrener. In the passage in question, Susana playfully threatens Luis with telling their parents about his feelings for Devlin, the American captain. In the revised version of the manuscript, Luis reveals to Susana that he is aware of her love for an Anglo captain, but Susana does not tease Luis about his own affection for another man. The deleted part reads as follows: "'You want to tease me, Luis, but I don't even want to listen. I'll tell her [mama] you're in love.' She laughed, hurried into the house."[7] This sentence does not appear in the published version of *Caballero*.

If we do read Caballero as a national romance, as many critics have suggested, then it follows that we must not overlook the major narrative plot involving the queer national romance between the Mexicano, Luis Gonzaga, and the Americano, Captain Devlin. If other parts marked for deletion by the authors were included by the editors for "narrative flow" or for their "ideological import," then we should certainly consider the narrative and ideological import of this deleted sentence regarding Gonzaga's attraction to Devlin.

To learn more about González's own desire to construct a queer Mexican American text, we can turn to her own archives. Several researchers have been interested in finding out exactly who Raleigh was, where she was from, and her cultural background in order to understand her coauthorship with González. But something in my initial exploration of González's work set off what I call my "intellectual gaydar." I began to wonder at the nature of the relationship between the two women coauthors, partly because of the continued confusion concerning their collaboration, the suppression of their work by González's husband Mireles, and the significant portion of their novel dedicated to telling the story of a same-sex relationship between a Mexican and an Anglo.

As I delved further into González's archives at Texas A&M University–Corpus Christi, I focused my search on correspondence between the coauthors. My other goal was to determine if González's well-documented ethnographic research on South Texas folklore included any stories of gay characters upon which the novel's Luis might be based, a strategy she employed for the development of many of her fictional characters. The most fruitful documents from this particular search included a couple of letters from Eimer to González. Over time, and after Eimer moved away from Texas, it seems that González wrote back to Eimer less frequently, and as a result Eimer's letters to González grew increasingly odd and desperate for González's attention (saying things like "have you dropped me out of your life" and "I miss how we were").[8] Eimer's letters can be interpreted as love letters to González, with Eimer wondering if González still loved her. Based on these findings, I suggest that their collaboration was quite queer and that we can productively interpret the act of these two women coauthoring an interracial historical romance as a queer erotic practice.

To be clear, my queer reading of González here is not necessarily about discovering if the author was in fact queer or lesbian as we understand that now but rather about opening up her work to queer lines of inquiry. I want to use this as an opportunity to pose questions about how we come to know or construct a queer Mexican American text. What does it mean to allow ourselves our queer desire for a text? What does it look like to be in search of a queer borderlands history? How might we broaden the way we construct new knowledge when we recover texts? "Lost" manuscripts may result not just from misplaced, suppressed, destroyed, or otherwise lost papers but also from people's lost experiences and lost lives, lives and knowledge that may have been lost to them and may be lost to us. Yet, what productive new knowledge can we construct from what we may never know of our own histories, literatures, and queer cultures?

In posing such questions, I wish to elucidate the *potentially* radical queer love that effervesces throughout and potentially around the text. I emphasize "potentially" here because in the novel, queer love is proffered as a potentiality. And in reading González and Raleigh's collaboration as a potentially radical queer love in its time and place, I mean to emphasize its retroactive potentiality.

As noted, many critics have categorized *Caballero* as a historical romance. Others have described it as an ethnographic novel. Some simply refer to it as a historical novel. Based on such a range of descriptors, we can gather that *Caballero* may be one and all of these. The novel—despite its blurring of ethnography, the novelistic form, historical fiction, and romance—depicts the "marriage" of two cultures, so understandably it is the novel's romance factor that dominates critical discussions. Yet, it remains unclear why Susana's romantic plot supersedes discussions of the novel if Luis's romantic plot parallels Susana's throughout most of the narrative. Perhaps Sedgwick's notion of effeminophobia can provide a useful framework for understanding this critical oversight. In *Tendencies*, Sedgwick astutely asserts that "[t]o begin to theorize gender and sexuality as distinct though intimately entangled axes of analysis has been, indeed, a great advance of recent lesbian and gay thought" (156). She goes on to explain that "[t]here is danger, however, that that advance may leave the effeminate boy once more in the position of the haunting abject—this time the haunting abject of gay thought itself" (156). To some degree, John Rechy's gay Chicano fiction has become a kind of haunting abject within Chicanx studies, as his work holds a contentious and uncertain place within some nodes of Chicanx critical thought. Rechy's overt queerness was later eclipsed by the conservative literary antics of Richard Rodríguez and the emergence of a formidable body of Chicana lesbiana literature in the 1980s. Within the *Caballero* narrative, the effeminate artist figure skirts close to becoming the haunting abject, that which cannot abide within the Mexicano familial and ranching structure as it desperately seeks to survive in the face of the U.S./Americano takeover.

Luis's ejection from his father's ranch borders between self-exile and forced expulsion but ultimately writes the queer out of Mexico and into the United States. Luis, then, becomes a figure of queer migration. In *Queer Migrations*, Lionel Cantú reflects on his experience of being called upon as an expert witness in a case in which Mexican gay men were seeking asylum in the United States based on their sexual orientation. Cantú posits that these scenes of legal negotiation mobilized sympathy from the courts through reinscribing two overlapping cultural assumptions. The first assumption put into play was that effeminized gay Mexicans were simultaneously considered shameful for their lack of proper masculinity and in need of protection by the state as persecuted or endangered subjects. The second assumption at work was that the relative freedom proffered by the United States rested on the "colonialist and racialist" ideas that the country affords its (sexual) citizens better protections (under the law), while the Mexican government continues to subject its citizens to an old-world regime of sexual control, particularly its darker-skinned, poorer, more indigenous populations. The corollary notion here is that the United States does not admit its own engagement in racializing or racially discriminating against (or even among) its citizen-subjects. For Luis in *Caballero*, the United States is the place for the liberated sexual subject, where a range of masculinities, including effeminacy, can exist. Luis seeks a kind of gay cultural asylum in the United States and achieves, or at least pursues, a queer American dream.

A recurring image in the novel is that of Don Santiago surveying his land and declaring to himself "All this is mine." In fact, the phrase "All This is Mine" was González's original title for the manuscript (Cotera, *Native Speakers*, 255, note 1). The final scene depicts the patriarch dying alone on a hill overlooking his ranch, his arms outstretched and empty. Does the irony of "all this is mine" go beyond the patriarch's demise and loss of all he believes is his? Given that the macho brother Alvaro is killed by Texas Rangers and the patriarch Don Santiago dies, leaving his ranch presumably to his daughters, who have both married Anglo U.S. military officers, Luis remains, despite his absence in the end, the sole figure of the Mexican ranchero—the *caballero*. The titular claim of "all this is mine" may signal a final attempt by Jovita González to stake her literal claim to sole, or at least primary, authorship with her collaborator. "All this is mine," as Don Santiago's legacy, may also be the sentiment of the emergent artistic antiranchero/antihero in the effeminately queer figure of Luis Gonzaga, who upon the death of the Mexican patriarch can finally imagine all of this—Mexico and America—to be his.

In the case of Jovita González's historical novel *Caballero,* the text attempts to resist not only U.S. hegemonic constructions of American history but also Mexican American patriarchal containment of the queer artist, as exemplified by the fictional character of Luis Gonzaga as well as the potentially queer artistic author González herself. Thus, through the character of the queer artist who resists patriarchal control of his gendered and racialized sexuality, González's novelistic commitment to queerness ultimately situates her work as a contribution not just to American literature and not just to a Chicana literary archive but also to a decidedly *queer* Chicana literary archive. Reading Jovita González's *Caballero* as an early queer Chicana novel demonstrates how the author's work prefigured the concerns of not just Chicana lesbian feminists in the late twentieth century but also contemporary Chicana writers concerned with questions of gender variance.

Conclusion

From a Long Line of Marimachas

It was el Día de los Muertos (Day of the Dead), and around thirty of us were crammed into a small cinder block meeting room at allgo in in Austin, Texas. Las Krudas Cubensi opened with an Afro-Latin@ drum rhythm.[1] After the musical introduction by Las Krudas, writer Fatima Mann performed her spoken word poetry. Her performance paid tribute not only to the dead but also to leaving things behind, killing off parts of ourselves or our lives that have caused us harm. When it was my turn to speak, I read from the works of Ana Sisnett, Chinwe Odeluga, Vincent Woodard, and Raúl R. Salinas, four poets of color who wrote prolifically yet left so much unwritten. Sisnett, Odeluga, and Woodard were queer activists and writers of color who left indelible marks on the LGBTQ+ community of central Texas. Salinas was a formidable Xicanindio poet and activist who was not queer-identified but grew over the years to become a staunch ally to queer people of color and a collaborator with allgo.

While I read, behind me stood a large altar filled with photos and mementos. Stacked on the altar were copies of books and poems by each of the writers lost too soon. Rather than read from my own poetry, I chose to read aloud a poem by Ana Sisnett, who for many years had been known to electrify allgo events with her fiercely erotic poetry infused with images of women loving women and her beloved home country of Panama. To close the program, Priscilla Hale, allgo's director and Ana's former partner, spoke to the audience about how the organization had been celebrating the Day of the Dead since the 1980s. The allgo organization began as the Austin Latina/o Lesbian Gay Organization when several members of the community got together to discuss how to respond to the growing HIV/AIDS crisis. allgo's initial focus centered on community organizing, health education, and culturally relevant programming to support people living with HIV and AIDS. While the organization has since expanded to become a Texas statewide queer people of color organization, allgo strives to maintain the Day of the Dead tradition. For the annual event, the organization builds a community altar decorated with artifacts honoring members of the community who have died, with visitors adding their own mementos.

Hale pointed out that honoring the dead for queer people can be especially complex when death brings out heteronormative and homophobic family members who might try to sweep evidence of queer lives under the rug. Hale mentioned members of the local community who had been out and proud community advocates, but upon their deaths the families who had legal power to manage their funerals took their bodies home and refused to acknowledge their queerness in obituaries and memorial services. Hale asked that we honor these lost individuals and avoid de-queering their legacies for the comfort of their families. "We are queer even in death," Hale insisted.

There were many new faces in the crowd, including young people who had recently moved to town. There were also people who had been attending allgo events for thirty years.[2] After gazing at the photos on the community altar, I recalled many of the same people assembling to pay tribute over the years to so many other queers of color lost:

Gloria Anzaldúa, 61, diabetes (1942–2004)
Boyd Vance, 48, aneurysm (1957–2005)
Vincent Woodard, 37, complications from HIV/AIDS, (1971–2008)
Ana Sisnett, 56, cancer (1952–2009)
Camile Pawha, 34, cancer (1975–2010)
Norma Hurtado, 24, murdered (1986–2011)

Whether through disease or violence, the queers for whom we had gathered had experienced what many considered early death. How do we calculate the effects of racism, sexism, classism, ableism, and homophobia on the course of their lives? Consider Ruth Wilson Gilmore's definition of racism and compound it with the other isms that interlock to foreclose possibilities: Gilmore defines racism as "the state-sanctioned and/or legal production and exploitation of group-differentiated vulnerabilities to premature death, in distinct yet densely interconnected political geographies" (261). As Joanna Brooks notes, "Gilmore's definition is pivotal in that it focuses not on how race is imagined or intended by white people but rather on how it is experienced by people of color. People of color experience racism as a set of political and economic conditions that compromise the quality or the longevity of their lives. The word 'vulnerability' seems to me to convey quite powerfully the compound quotidian costs of survival under these political conditions" (313). Each of the folks listed above as among the lost, in varying ways, engaged in practices that challenged gender and sexuality norms and also challenged the very political conditions that marked people like them as members of vulnerable populations.

With each loss experienced during my visioning of this project, the literary analytics and ideas began to take on a more potent urgency for me. I began to alternate between doubting and clinging to the potentialities of theorizing queer living through queer literatures. How might literature illuminate and challenge the normative structures and social formations that constrict and threaten to cut short such fabulous queer people in their fabulous queer lives? How might queer texts open up new ways of imagining queer lives and gender variant possibilities?

With each subsequent loss of a queer writer of color after Anzaldúa, I recalled Cherríe Moraga's asking at Anzaldúa's Austin memorial "Who's next?" Although Moraga meant who is the next writer who will have a strong effect, as did Anzaldúa, I also heard in her question a lamentation of the repeated losses of queer lives extinguished too soon, a sentiment certainly palpable to the many writers and activists in the room who had lived through the deaths of many friends in the devastating HIV/AIDS epidemic. Moraga's question invoked the title of her prose and poetry collection *The Last Generation*, published by the feminist collective South End Press in 1993.

Moraga dedicates her collection of prose and poetry "[t]o honor the legacies of Audre Lorde and César Chávez" and "*[f]or the yet unborn*" (author's emphasis, n.p.). Thus, Moraga cites multiple legacies of social movements. She calls on the legacies of the renowned black Caribbean American writer Audre Lorde, who self-identified as "black, lesbian, mother, warrior, poet" and died in 1992, and the Chicano movement labor organizer César Chávez, who died in 1993. Moraga simultaneously suggests that she does indeed imagine and hope for a next generation to come in "the yet unborn."

Despite this initial glimmer of hope, Moraga makes it clear that her work emanates from her fear of the finality of imperial conquest. She writes that "[i]n 1524, just three years after the Spanish Conquest of the Aztec Empire, the Náhuatl sages, the tlamatinime, came before the missionary friars in defense of their religion. 'Our gods are already dead,' they stated. 'Let us perish now.' Their codices lay smoldering in heaps of ash" (2). Moraga then identifies herself as operating within this legacy of the conquered Aztecs:

> I write with the same knowledge, the same sadness, recognizing the full impact of the colonial 'experiment' on the lives of Chicanos, mestizos, and Native Americans. Our codices—dead leaves unwritten—lie smoldering in the ashes of disregard, censure, and erasure. *The Last Generation* emerges from those ashes. I write it against time, out of a sense of urgency that Chicanos are a disappearing tribe, out of a sense of this disappearance in my own familia. (2)

Moraga's fear of Chicanxs disappearing from within her own family is partly borne of her own mixed-race identity of Chicana and Anglo. The fear of losing Chicanidad or Chicanxness within her own family extends outward to a globalized fear of total assimilation and erasure of Chicanxs by absorption into the dominant

Anglo culture. This fear of destruction or conquest is compounded by rejection by potential community allies, as Moraga details her own personal rejection as a Chicana lesbian by traditional Chicanxs as well as by white lesbian feminists. Furthermore, she connects the struggles of Chicana lesbians to those of gay Chicanos, particularly around the impacts of HIV and AIDS: "The AIDS epidemic has seriously shaken the foundation of the Chicano gay community" (162). As a result, argues Moraga, "[Chicano] gay men seem more willing than ever to explore those areas of political change that will ensure their survival." According to Moraga, "In their fight against AIDS, they have been rejected and neglected by both the white gay male establishment and the Latino heterosexual health-care community. They have also witnessed direct support by Latina lesbians" (163).

Moraga claims that the ultimate struggle for lesbian and gay Chicanxs and for Chicanxs in general is aligned with the struggles of native peoples across the globe, citing the fight for self-sovereignty as a shared struggle. Yet, in Moraga's estimation, the dilemma of Chicanxs is exacerbated by the fact that many Chicanxs have turned away from or ignored the knowledge of their indigenous elders. Moraga ends *The Last Generation* by urging a "new Chicano nationalism" and by naming queer Chicanas as inheritors of "La Causa Chicana," as a form of hope for Chicanxs to survive into the next millennium.

The Last Generation includes an essay titled "Queer Aztlán: The Re-formation of the Chicano Tribe" in which Moraga lays out a vision for a future homeland for Chicanx queers. Significantly, she first presented a version of the "Queer Aztlán" essay at the first national conference of the Latino/a Lesbian and Gay Organization (LLEGO), held in Houston in 1992. LLEGO, which unfortunately disbanded due to funding issues several years ago, formed as an offshoot of Austin's allgo. The place and impetus for Moraga's proposing a "queer Aztlán," then, occurred within the context of the first nationally organized gathering of queer Chicanxs and Latinxs.

Moraga's conception of a "queer Aztlán" offers an alternative vision to the fear of cultural destruction expressed throughout much of *The Last Generation*. It also serves as a mixed retort to the radical Queer Nation, a New York–based group formed in 1990 to mobilize controversial direct actions against homophobia; the group was criticized by mainstream media for its daring tactics, such as outing public figures. Groups such as Queer Nation were also criticized by queer people of color for not including them. Arguing from the get-go for another way of making change, Moraga opens *The Last Generation* with an epigraph quoting Mexican novelist Rosario Castellanos: "Debe haber otro modo . . . / Otro modo de ser humano y libre / Otro modo de ser" (There must be another way . . . / Another way to be human and free / Another way to be).

In my investigation of post-borderlands Chicana literature, gender variant critique proposes un otro modo de ser. The archive I have assembled here argues for an understanding of the centrality of gender variant critique in Chicana literature. In fact, although I focus on what I have called the post-borderlands, indicating work that takes up but goes beyond Anzaldúan theory and approaches, one can trace thinking about gender variance in Anzaldúa's own unpublished body of work.

Even those deeply familiar with Anzaldúa's work might be surprised by some of the artifacts gathered in her archive.[3] In some of her unpublished manuscripts, some of which are quite explicitly erotic,[4] Anzaldúa attempts to explore writing gender against and beyond the gender binary in ways signaled by ideas she mentions in her published work. In "Turning Points," an interview with Anzaldúa that Linda Smuckler conducted in *Interviews/Entrevistas*, Anzaldúa mentions a novella she was writing while in graduate school. She describes having written the piece for a class assignment: "For the Poetry of Decadence class, I wrote a story about two Chicano maricones and Andrea. She was cousin to Joaquín, one of the main characters, and brother to Heche (He/she), the novella's protagonist. I put all the decadent elements I could into the story" (24). The "Heche" story Anzaldúa refers to is now in her papers archived at the Benson Latin American Collection at the University of Texas at Austin.[5] A folder containing the story has

Oct. 22, 1975
Rough draft

```
                From the GLASS Periphery By the
        Hole of the (White) Apocalyptic Ojo (I ) He
                        Says Never

                           By


                     Gloria Anzaldúa

            "And owls shall dwell there, and satyrs
            shall dance there."--Isaiah 13:21

             I've been trying to see him for weeks.  Through the
    front door, at first, with El Guero's naked eye looking at me
    through the eyehole in the door, then his face, there, above
    me, resolute, his blondness heightened by the dark, impenetrable
    door.  (Juan Q.              won't be still, as if his words
    will keep death away,              of the past, of our
    childhood--that Heche has only one servant, that Heche has
    into his snell.)
```

FIGURE 6. First page of an unpublished manuscript from the Gloria Evangelina Anzaldúa Papers. Nettie Lee Benson Latin American Collection, University of Texas Libraries, University of Texas at Austin. Copyright by The Gloria Evangelina Anzaldúa Literary Trust. May not be duplicated without permission from the Trust.

several handwritten drafts with varying titles, including "Where Owls Dwell and Satyrs Dance" and "From the Glass Periphery by the Hole of the (White) Apocalyptic Ojo (I) He Says Never" (Figure 6). Some versions include an accented letter in "Heché," and others do not. The alternate titles point to Anzaldúa's interest in rethinking the borderlands between human and nonhuman species and various forms or states of consciousness, interests that pervade her book *Borderlands/La Frontera* as well.

While Anzaldúa's unpublished archival materials contain highly problematic conceptions of intersex and gender variance by contemporary understandings, what I want to highlight here in her manuscript is her desire to think beyond a fixed gender dichotomy more directly than in her more well-known works. The

"Heche" story in particular demonstrates Anzaldúa's desire to use fiction as an avenue for thinking through fantasies of gender and gender shifting. "Heche" seems to tell the story of a protagonist of undetermined gender and a circle of friends involved in political activism and making theater. The story has dreamlike scenes in which reality and dream states blur, and it becomes difficult for the protagonist—and the reader—to follow who inhabits which body or realm.

The "Heche" manuscript contains the author's handwritten markup and revision notes, leaving parts of the story unclear or seemingly in process. Based on the extant copy, Anzaldúa intended for the story to explore a mixing and disrupting of genders, bodies, and literary strategies. It could be read alongside her borderlands thinking in which Anzaldúa relates the concept of being "half and half" in terms of race as a mestiza to being a mezcla of gender. In the iconic poem "To Live in the Borderlands Means You . . . ," the poem's persona says that the mestiza in the borderlands is the "forerunner of a new race, / half and half—both woman and man, neither—/a new gender" (*Borderlands/La Frontera* 216). In other published writings, she uses the term "mitad" (half) to describe this mix. In a keynote titled "Bridge, Drawbridge, Sandbar, or Island: Lesbians-of-Color Hacienda Alianzas," Anzaldúa calls herself a "mestiza queer person" and says that she looks around the audience for "the other half and half's, mita' y mita' (as queer women are called in South Texas)" (*The Gloria Anzaldúa Reader* 141). As AnaLouise Keating mentions in the text's footnote, "mita' y mita'" is short for "mitad y mitad," reflecting Anzaldúa's South Texas pronunciation.

Although many cite Anzaldúa's work, and her borderlands theory in particular, most focus on Anzaldúa's take on the inter-section of race, class, gender, and sexuality, while discussions of the gendered aspects of her work often focus on her identity as a woman without exploring possibilities for genderqueerness. Her use of "both woman and man, neither" is strikingly similar to contemporary definitions of genderqueer. To be clear, I am not suggesting that Anzaldúa's mitad y mitad refers to a genderqueer or transgender identity. And of course, being transgender or gen-derqueer are not about half and half.[6] In *Borderlands/La Frontera,* Anzaldúa theorizes how borderland inhabitants develop facility with transcending the limiting constructs imposed on them by systems that demand that they choose sides in an either/or world, and "half and half" offers another term for her to think through processes of coming to consciousness and moving across and through borders. Anzaldúa did not identify as transgender, but she expressed a sense of dislocation and unbelonging in relation to normative gender. With her assertion of being mitad y mitad, Anzaldúa disidentified with the gender binary in a way that lends itself to gender variant possibilities.[7]

"Heche" begins with a biblical epigraph from Isaiah 13:21 that reads "And owls shall dwell there, and satyrs shall dance there." The narrator is searching for a way into a guarded house where a shape-shifting person lives but fears being duped by the being. We learn that the narrator runs a theater company in Austin and that the shape-shifter has money needed to save the failing theater company. Once inside the house, the narrator experiences a series of mysterious events in various rooms that change color and shape. The encounters between the narrator, the shape-shifter, and other characters are charged with erotic energy.

One of the many intriguing aspects of the manuscript is its references to drugs as a tool for altering one's sense of reality, which Anzaldúa spoke openly about in interviews. In an interview, she recounts a time in which she experienced herself as having many parts or selves, as being "multiple" (*Interviews/Entrevistas* 36). Anzaldúa says that this experience occurred while she "was writing the novella about Heche, el maricón, for [her] decadent class" and that she planned to incorporate her visual experience into the writing. She says that "I was tripping on mushrooms. . . . I was going to take stream-of-consciousness, but rather than just narrate an inner stream-of-consciousness I would include what was happening externally. Heche goes through things in his head and his body ritually, but it's all situated in a physical reality. Instead of a series of monologues or ideas and images, they'd be a series of visual—like scenes in a movie" (36). The "Heche" story in the archive includes what appear to be descriptions of hallucinations in which bodies morph between human and nonhuman and across gender distinctions.

Near the story in her papers, Anzaldúa had handwritten notes about various cinema techniques, and she seemed to be interested in exploring those in this narrative. The surreal scenes show Anzaldúa's interest not only in experimental narrative writing but also in using fiction to contemplate her ideas about transformations, both bodily and psychic. In the "Heche" draft, bodies transform between and across genders and species. In an interview by Keating, Anzaldúa discusses her fascination with "shapeshifting," the notion that people could transform into animal shapes (*Interviews/Entrevistas* 283).

The narrator initially tries unsuccessfully to break into the shape-shifter's glass house, where "[n]o one leaves" and "[n]o one goes in." After finding a way in and being led to psychedelic rooms, the narrator unveils a vast medicinal collection. The narrator names a detailed list of herbs such as a curandera (folk healer) might posses, along with a range of drugs such as marijuana, cocaine, and peyote and various "aphrodisiac concoctions." The host takes the narrator to a room with a film collection and proceeds to show a variety of pornographic films. The narrator becomes immersed as a "participant in a sex dimension sport where penises and buttocks and mouths are magnified out of proportion, the cruising and the tricking, en travesti, voyeuristic camp-queen madness and falsetto raving, biing [*sic*] blown, the plunge and the recoil and on the other screens a double projection of separate films running simultaneously." As the scene progresses, it becomes less clear whether the narrator is merely watching or is having sex with the host and other unnamed people.

What may seem surprising to some because it was not her modus operandi in her major works is Anzaldúa's incorporation of men's bodies, sex between men, and sex among myriad sexes, genders, and bodies. The characters engage in an orgy, and bodies seem to meld into each other. Critic Suzanne Bost describes Anzaldúa as a writer "who embraced corporeal, national, and identitarian permeability" ("Unsafe Politics and Risky Connections" 127), and this permeability is clearly evident here. Given Anzaldúa's propensity for the autobiographical, one might assume that the first-person narrator in her fiction is a woman based on Anzaldúa herself. However, the narrator describes having a penis, though it is unclear how the narrator identifies. And although the character Heche is also described as "he" and as having a penis, it is unclear from the dialogue how the character himself might identify. The name Heche confounds attempts to place the character on one side of a sex or gender binary. In an interview with Smuckler, Anzaldúa explained that story's title as referring to "He/she," a pejorative term for a transgender person. It seems that Anzaldúa uses "He/she" uncritically, and it is unclear whether she was aware of its negative connotations.

Anzaldúa also explores ideas about gender variance and intersex bodies in a poem titled "Intersex—Breast with Penis" in her archives. In this unpublished poem, the speaker describes their experience as "[a] woman locked up in a man's body that's [sic] how I've / always felt ever since I was 6 or 7." The poem goes on to speak of "[h]ormone shots, the/operations the pain." The speaker says that "[f]or a long time I felt suspended / breast with penis then no penis, no vagina shaved my / arms permed my hair as I waited for the change." While these kinds of limiting images of intersex would not find an uncritical audience in today's more savvy and inclusive LGBTQ+ publics, Anzaldúa's archival articulations point to how she was imagining gender variance as among the many vectors she engaged in her work prior to, in, and beyond *Borderlands/La Frontera*. Anzaldúa was interested in gender variance as a way to imagine and represent Chicanx queerness and gender nonconformity beyond existing borders and boundaries of the time.

Gender variant critique continues to be relevant in conversation with writings in the contemporary context. Emerging writer Claire M. Jackson, who identifies as "a 30-something Hispanic transwoman (read as: MtF Transsexual)" ("About Claire de Lunacy" n.p.), is the author of the 2012 short story "Camille," which centers a transwoman character as she negotiates the threat of violence from her friend's husband. Like Anzaldúa's unpublished "Heche," Jackson's story contributes to an archive of Chicana texts examining the borders of gender. They each engage in their own forms of interrogation of the gender binary albeit from different angles and approaches.

Jackson's story casts a trans woman, Camille, as the friend of a presumably cisgender woman named Sara, who is married to an abusive, presumably cisgender man named Scott. The brief story begins with a description of Scott's displeasure at his wife's friendship with a transgender woman and ends with Camille's response to Scott's violence.

The narrative contrasts Scott's confusion about and hostility toward Camille's gender against the other characters' genders, which are unmarked and hence presumably cisgender. The story uses "she" to refer to the wife Sara and "he" to refer to the husband Scott, setting them up as a "properly" gendered heterosexual couple. Camille is identified as a trans woman through a series of insults directed her way by Scott. Through Scott's antagonism, the narrative emphasizes how Camille's difference is something remarkable in that it must be remarked upon by Scott. Jackson characterizes Scott's violence as common and mundane: "He was a monster of the ordinary sort: violent, prone to drunken excess and stupendous rage" ("Camille" n.p.). His concern about Camille's influence on Sara revolves around her encouraging Sara to reject Scott's domineering behavior: "[I]t was like she was transfusing steel into his wife's brittle frame." Camille's boldness begins to anger Scott more and more, and eventually Sara divorces Scott.

By situating the three characters within the domestic space and subjecting the two women, one cisgender and one transgender, to verbal abuse—and the threat of physical abuse—by a man, the story renders transmisogyny visible as a form of misogyny, perpetuated by the dangerous linkage between hegemonic masculinity and antiwoman violence. Scott refers to Camille as "no woman, not natural-born at least," and as "a trans-whatever." Scott refuses to accept Camille's gender identity as valid, claiming that she cannot be a woman and mocking the term "transgender." He recalls his father's advice given to him on his wedding day, encouraging him to "knock some sense into" women.

Although the story does not specify the characters' racial-ethnic identities, the spelling of the wife's name, Sara, can be interpreted as the name's Spanish pronunciation. The word "brown" is used in an odd way to describe Sara's looks, with an emphasis on her aging and the accumulative effect of abuse on her body: "her beauty not yet faded but starting to brown at the edges with constant fear." With Scott described as "The Man," perhaps associating him with whiteness, and Sara as possibly Latina, we can read them as figuring a colonizer-colonized trope, a racialized gendered dynamic that will be interrupted by the intervention of Camille, of unknown racial-ethnic identity but perhaps Latina as well.

After Sara ends her marriage with Scott, Scott goes to Camille's home to try to physically attack her with a tire iron. Camille seizes the tire iron and crushes it into dust. She reveals that her name is "not really Camille; it's Camael," an avenging archangel figure. As her wings and armor become visible, she quips, "I don't wear the helmet anymore, it's hell on my hair." The story ends with Camille/Camael telling the surprised Scott, "Now let's see if we can knock some sense into you, shall we?" Camille/Camael outwits the "monster of the ordinary sort," transforming the near trans bashing into a heroic trans vision of smashing the patriarch(y). Camille confronts Scott not with his own weapon, which she has rendered obsolete, but instead with the full force of her presence as a literal avenging angel. Scott's targeting of both his wife Sara and her transgender friend Camille stresses that the pressure to define one's gender according to normative expectations can be dangerous and can be enforced by physical violence, in this case gendered violence targeting women, including trans women. The story contemplates the many kinds of violence faced by women and gender variant people, and the narrative models a transfeminist[8] approach to liberation. By drawing on the trope of the violent gender variant character to offer up a revenge fantasy, the story imagines a form of solidarity, albeit through the use of physical force, between cisgender women and trans women.

Gender variant critique is relevant for and in dialogue with trans analytics. Francisco Galarte points out that because "trans* folk easily confound gender binaries that remain rigidly ingrained in even the most recent queer Chican@ scholarship, 'transgender' presents an important challenge to current paradigms for theorizing racialized and gendered sexualities in jotería studies" (230). Calling for the need to take trans seriously within Chicanx studies, Galarte says that he is "asserting the indispensability of trans-analytics to the aim and scope of jotería studies as a critical project" (233).[9] Like Galarte, I see the development of a more expansive gender critical approach such as gender variant critique as participating in "a refusal to be silent about the myriad ways that racialized and gendered violence makes itself known across the complex and multiple manifestations and iterations of queer and trans* that constitute Chican@" (233). Gender variant critique offers a mode of analysis that regards genderqueerness and gender nonconformity, while they may be used by some as identity categories, as having the potential for informing interpretive frameworks for analyzing and dismantling sex/gender binaries. To be clear, I do not mean to conflate categories such as queer and trans or assume any particular identity-related category, such as trans or genderqueer, to be the be-all/end-all umbrella under which other identities or analytics should coalesce. Rather, a gender variant approach allows for broader consideration of the wide range of possible and seemingly impossible genders and ways of embodying, self-describing, and theorizing gender nonconforming, transgender, genderqueer, queerly gendered, queer, marimacha, and other existing and not yet known gender variant embodiments and experiences.

Championing gender variant critique in post-borderlands Chicana literature is part of a larger commitment to the ongoing utility of intersectionality. In Kimberlé Crenshaw's original positing of the theory of intersectionality, she was speaking not only of black women as individuals with intersecting identities but also of systems, intersectional social structures that constrictively organize black women's lives and constrain them to one category at a time. Intersectionality has since been widely extended to inform women of color feminisms.[10] While intersectionality has been taken up by many as a crucial tool for feminist theory, ongoing debates continue to swirl around whether the concept continues to be useful. According to Vivian May, "While intersectionality has been widely influential, its approach to subjectivity, knowledge, power, and social systems has also encountered quite a degree of resistance and continues to do so" (1). Jennifer C. Nash remarks that "[f]eminist debates around intersectionality—which I term the intersectionality wars—have become particularly and peculiarly contentious" (117). The many reductive takes on intersectionality referenced by May and Nash do not necessarily signal a failure of intersectional theory itself but rather symptoms of how disciplining social systems under racial capitalism seek to simplify the categorizing of subjects for the state's ease and for the sake of maintaining hegemony. Though some critics of intersectionality may regard the concept as relying too much on notions of identity, this should not limit intersectionality's continued imaginative possibilities as long as we do not remain fixated on identities themselves as fixed or ossifying categories or as the sole locus of intersectionality. Locating intersections within the individual falsely limits the purview of intersectionality. The focus on intersectional identity, or intersectionality as merely identity, is a common misapplication of the theory, reducing a cross section of a person's social locations to stand in for the whole.

Sandra K. Soto, in *Reading Chican@ Like a Queer*, suggests that intersectionality is too inflexible and limiting, "perhaps too spatially rigid and exacting a metaphor to employ when considering the ever dynamic and unending processes of subject formation" (6). Soto argues for wordiness, against "look[ing] for a shorthand for naming or understanding or footnoting the confounding manifold ways that our bodies, our work, our desires are relentlessly interpellated by unequivalent social processes" (6). Central to her thinking here is the suggestion "that race, sexuality, and gender are much too complex, unsettled, porous (and I do mean to be wordy here), mutually constitutive, unpredictable, incommensurable, and dynamic, certainly too spatially and temporally contingent, *ever* (even if only for an instant) to travel independently of one another. But they would have to do so in order to be conceived of as intersecting" (6). Soto's call to think dynamically about race, sexuality, and gender is important to heed. Yet, if we presume that race, sexuality, and gender must travel separately in the intersection, we may miss other possibilities. While the metaphor of an intersection does seem to imply separate axes, Crenshaw's original formulation of intersectionality as a legal strategy requires us to think of more than one identity category existing together simultaneously and continuously. Intersectionality can be imagined and deployed in such a way as to allow for matrices of complex interpellations.

Vivian May's most recent book, *Pursuing Intersectionality, Unsettling Dominant Imaginaries,* analyzes the extent of what she describes as a backlash against intersectionality in feminist thinking. As May points out, "We must question why intersectionality is misconstrued as endorsing essentialist identity models or political approaches, caricatured as a narrow lens focused 'only' on Black women and solely on 'oppression' (the two are often homogenized and conflated), or used by practitioners in ways that uphold single-axis thinking, rather than align with its matrix orientation" (ix). Indeed, in taking up critiques of intersectionality, we need to be mindful of not performing antiblackness. Chicanx studies cannot afford to divest itself from intersectionality, partly because it still has potential for pushing our thinking and partly because this theory has been one of the bridges that has allowed us to develop complex approaches to Chicanx studies and social movements. Without the theorizing of the Combahee River Collective, we may not have had *This Bridge Called My Back.*[11] However, the crossover or mainstreaming success of intersectionality has led to a reification of the term that too often focuses on individual intersectional subjects and risks an additive "diversity" approach. It is often the misuse of intersectionality that gives rise to a sense that it is time to move on from this metaphor, and theorists' work with assemblages, affect theory, poststructuralist, and other endeavors may offer their own variations and engagement with how to work ourselves out of some of intersectionality's perceived impasses.

At the same time that some are calling for a theoretical shift away from or beyond intersectionality, contemporary political movements such as Black Lives Matter and indigenous coalitions of water protectors claim intersectionality as a core element of their praxis. Patrisse Cullors, one of the cofounders of the Black Lives Matters movement, says that intersectionality "should be the basis on which we understand how we organize" because "[w]e are not one-dimensional" (Butterworth n.p.), and the Indigenous Coalition at Standing Rock put forth a call to "unleash a global *intersectional* resistance to fossil fuels and fascism" ("#NoDAPL Last Stand Call to Action!" n.d.). These moves suggest that the theory of intersectionality maintains a complex political utility for movements that confront white supremacy, colonialism, imperialism, capitalism, and state-sanctioned violence against black, brown, and indigenous peoples. Academic calls to move away from intersectionality should pause to consider intersectionality's on-the-ground mobilizations during this particular political moment when rising movements led by black, brown, and indigenous public intellectuals and organizers call for taking up intersectionality in praxis.[12]

Jasbir Puar acknowledges the limits of the current identitarian understandings of intersectionality, advancing instead the alternative conception of assemblages. In "Disability," Puar says that in thinking through the relationship between trans and disability, "[o]ften the intersectional subject gets tokenized or manipulated as a foil such that the presence of this subject actually then prohibits accountability toward broader alliances" (78). Here Puar cautions against the "liberal deployment of intersectionality, implicitly based on the assumption of the equality of each vector to the other and the absence of each in the other" (79–80). Puar raises the "question of what kinds of assemblages appear before and beyond intersectionality that might refuse to isolate trans and disability as separate and distinct conceptual entities" (78), and we can extend this question to other possible intersectional assemblages that may provide for gender variant critique. Puar's work has been taken up as a push away from intersectionality toward assemblages, though in "Intersectionality and Its Discontents" Nash says that she is "deeply suspicious of the reduction of Jasbir Puar's theorizing of assemblage to a critique of intersectionality (and sometimes *the* critique of intersectionality)" (117). As Puar reflects in *Terrorist Assemblages* on certain limited circumstances in which an intersectional approach or analysis may be "indispensible" (125), her work invites us to explore the possibilities that arise when we hold intersectionality and assemblages in our minds at once.

Tethering intersectionality to an understanding of individuals, subjects, and subject formation as well as social structures remains critical for not only interpreting existing structures but also imagining ways of dismantling and reconfiguring those structures and their attendant structures of thought. For productive ways to move through these debates and think through the potential of gender variant critique, we can turn to María Lugones's "Toward a Decolonial Feminism" for theorizations of the coloniality of gender, colonial difference, and the fractured locus as ways to apprehend structures as well as effects and the potential for responding to binaristic structures that perform colonial violence.[13] Lugones is interested not just in understanding how the "coloniality of gender" operates but also in imagining possibilities for "rejection, resistance, and response" (753). She says that "I can think of the self in relation as responding to the coloniality of gender at the colonial difference from a fractured locus, backed by an alternative communal source of sense that makes possible elaborate responses" (755). Dwelling on the fractured locus, per Lugones, does not merely allow us to build a feminist coalitional politics but does so by allowing us to think through the intersections of subjectivities and the structures that bind them. In this way, intersectionality can be attentive not just to the intersections of identities or structures but also to the fractured locus as the site where identities and structures intersect and collide and forms of resistance can become imagined as possible.[14] This aligns with May's contention that intersectionality draws on a "'both/and' worldview" (4). Like Lugones's moves toward decolonial feminism, gender variant critique seeks to undo the structures of thought that figure and violently impose gender in binaristic terms. As Emma Pérez stated in her keynote "The Will to Feel: Decolonial Anzaldúan Methods" at El Mundo Zurdo 2016, "Decolonial is not decolonial without a queer trans analytic." Gender variant critique and intersectionality are vital for reorganizing the structures of social systems to account for intersecting identities and experiences. For taking up gender variant critique, intersectionality remains a crucial analytic tool.

One place where gender variant critique's intersectional imperative is immediately visible is in the resolution of the case of the San Antonio Four. As I have maintained throughout this book, attending to questions of gender variance can have material implications on people's lives, as in the case of the San Antonio Four being persecuted not merely for being lesbians but also for exceeding the boundaries of gender conformity as well as the limits of Chicanidad. Artists, activists, and advocates have been involved in telling and rewriting the story of the San Antonio Four. Filmmaker Deborah Esquenazi took up their story in her documentary *Southwest of Salem*. The Innocence Project took on their case. They were released, and then their friends and family organized a campaign to raise funds to work toward their exoneration (Figures 7 and 8). The film went on tour, drawing attention to the exoneration campaign. The Texas Court of

FIGURE 7. Photograph of members of the San Antonio Four and their families celebrating upon learning of their exoneration. Copyright by Kin Man Hui/San Antonio Express-News via ZUMA Wire.

FIGURE 8. Photograph of a license plate celebrating the exoneration of the San Antonio Four. Copyright by Kin Man Hui/San Antonio Express-News via ZUMA Wire.

Criminal Appeals heard the case and issued a ruling exonerating all four women in November 2016. In the ruling opinion, Judge David Newell declared that "[t]hese women have carried that burden. They are innocent. And they are exonerated" (Zavala n.p.).

At work in the original trial were multiple regulating structures. Lesbophobia and homophobia allowed the jurors to construct the lesbian defendants as dangerously deviant, prone to violence, and queer threats to children.[15] Heterosexist and heteronormative thinking circumscribed the women as being available to and for men, their queerness rendering them impossible subjects in the courtroom. The women's information that the original accusations arose out of the girls' father's retaliation against one of the women for rebuffing his sexual advances was not considered meaningful testimony in the original trial. Gender normativity disallowed the defendants from being understood as trustworthy, and as Elvia Mendoza notes, as queerly gendered figures "their gender did not elicit compassion" (76). Racialized and elitist frameworks reduced the women to being disposable, untrustworthy, and suspect because of their statues as working-class Chicanas.

Their eventual exoneration was achieved in part because of the discounting of Dr. Nancy Kellogg's "expert" testimony at the original trial, which she had recanted due to new medical knowledge regarding physical evidence of sexual abuse. It is noteworthy, though Judge Newell's opinion does not note it, that Dr. Kellogg had also claimed at the original trial that the alleged abuse "could be satanic-related" (qtd. in Chammah n.p.). It is also important to note that Esquenazi's film does not merely document the case of the San Antonio Four; it also performs crucial cultural work. The film, with its gender variant critique, makes clear the intersections of oppression at work in the wrongful conviction. It also played a vital role in mobilizing a responsive audience around this critical issue, using intersectional thinking to raise public awareness and money for their legal defense fund. The final opinion of the Court of Criminal Appeals opens with a mention of Esquenazi's documentary about the case and the high-profile media the film received in publications such as *Rolling Stone* and the *Texas Tribune* (Court of Criminal Appeals of Texas 3). In reacting to the court ruling that exonerated the four women, declaring them completely innocent of any wrongdoing, Esquanazi said in an interview with *Corriente Latina* that "[t]his is a stunning victory, not only for the San Antonio Four, but for gay rights. . . . I couldn't have imagined that six years ago, with nothing more than a camera and shoe-leather journalistic persistence, that this day would come. It shows the power of art. It shows that even with no cultural capital, power, or resources, we can make great change" ("The San Antonio Four Are Declared Innocent and Fully Exonerated by the Texas Court of Criminal Appeals!"). Esquenazi's documentary enacts an intersectional and gender variant critique in ways that have had material consequences in the lives of the San Antonio Four. Although not every application of gender variant critique has such a direct material result, gender variant critique works toward extricating us from the regulatory social structures in which we are deeply imbricated. A gender variant approach provides an analytic tool for critiquing and potentially transforming those structures.

Gender variant critique exposes the structures of thought that render Chicanx gender variance unreadable and breaks open critical spaces for understanding, imagining, and living. Through my examination of Chicana cultural productions, it becomes clear that gender variance haunts the Chicana literary and cultural archive. In some cases I have examined here, gender variance is a direct presence, such as in Lemus's genderqueer and transgender novels; in others it may be located through gaps and queer excesses. Through analyzing performance, in the sense of theatrical performances such as those by Adelina Anthony as well as the daily performances subjected to state scrutiny in the case of the San Antonio Four, we can see how gender variant critique becomes key to broadening understandings of queer, transgender, and gender variant Chicana and Chicanx cultural productions. In postborderlandia, gender variant critique offers a perpetually unfolding map of liberatory potentialities.

Notes

Introduction

1. I use "Chicanx" as a more gender-inclusive and expansive term than "Chicano" or its variations. I explain this terminology in more detail later in this chapter.

2. In the essay "Thirty Years of Chicana/Latina Lesbian Literary Production," Alicia Gaspar de Alba describes contemporary Chicana/Latina literature as part of what she terms "Generation Q," which she marks within the time frame 2001 to 2011. According to Gaspar de Alba, "The gender-bending post-2000 Chican@ generation, building on the work of Chicana lesbian and Chicana feminist theorists from the 1980s, has turned the lens of gender and sexuality inward on the Chicano/a body, to further decolonize and deconstruct notions of the feminine/masculine, maleness/femaleness, and queerness/transgenderedness within Chicana lesbian and gay Chicano subjectivities, giving rise to new genders and sexual identities (e.g., bois, bears, MTFs/FTMs, female masculinity)" (471). Felicia Luna Lemus is among the handful of authors whom Gaspar de Alba designates as indicative of this "gender-bending" generation of literary output.

3. I use "heteronormative" to refer to the set of expectations and structures of enforcement that align with the assumption or enforcement of heterosexuality as the only acceptable or natural way of being. Laurent Berlant and Michael Warner, in "Sex in Public," explain the term "heternormativity" as follows: "By heteronormativity we mean the institutions, structures of understanding, and practical orientations that make heterosexuality seem not only coherent—that is, organized as a

sexuality—but also privileged" (548, note 2). They go on to say that "it consists less of norms that could be summarized as a body of doctrine than of a sense of rightness produced in contradictory manifestations— often unconscious, immanent to practice or to institutions." In *Fear of a Queer Planet,* Warner says that "even when coupled with a toleration of minority sexualities, heteronormativity can be overcome only by actively imagining a necessarily and desirably queer world" (xvi).

4. B. Aultman says that "a cisgender person's gender is on the same side as their birth-assigned sex, in contrast to which a transgender person's gender is on the other side (trans-) of their birth-assigned sex" ("Cisgender" 61). Suess, Espineira, and Walters assert that "the questioning of cis/heteronormativity and gender binarism, as well as the demand of a broader social recognition of gender/body diversity, is considered an important issue for all people" ("Depathologization" 75).

5. Luz Calvo and Catrióna Rueda Esquibel in "Our Queer Kin" state that "critically, queers demand an acknowledgment of transgender and gender queer to account for those who refuse or reoccupy the categories of male and female" (110).

6. Historian Yolanda Leyva notes that Anzaldúa "was unable to continue her graduate education because her fields of interest were considered unacceptable" (21).

7. allgo, founded in Austin, Texas, in 1985, was formerly called the Austin Latina/o Lesbian, Gay, Bisexual, and Transgender Organization, or ALLGO.

8. Coatlicue refers to the ancient Mexica goddess of birth and death.

9. See Anzaldúa's "Towards a New Consciousness" in *Borderlands/La Frontera* on how she imagines working as a means of liberation "[p]or la mujer de mi raza" (99).

10. I use the term "genderqueerness" to refer to conforming identities and gender expressions that trouble the feminine/masculine binary. I also suggest it has broader applications and potential as an analytic category.

11. For more on this point, see Linda Martín Alcoff's "The Unassimilated Theorist." Martín Alcoff says that "Anzaldúa's iconic status in feminism resulted in the contradiction of an iconoclast becoming the new standard. The status she attained in the nineties as the authentic voice of the multiply oppressed was often paradoxically used to provide an

epistemological foundation for antifoundationalist, postmodern theories. In other words, her work was used to bolster some of the exclusionary and elistist theoretical fashions of the very institution that made her marginal" (255–56).

12. For an analysis of "postnationalism," see Ellie D. Hernández's *Postnationalism in Chicana/o Literature and Culture*. Hernández states that "[b]ecause a stable gendered identity is next to impossible to categorize, particularly in a transnational economy, the work of the nation is to produce, regulate, and impose upon its citizens a national discourse that can be assimilated and reproduced. Under capitalism, however, what are the conditions that permit homosexuality to thrive? Queerness can be seen as the cultural attribute of homosexual life in which a nexus between race and ethnicity can finally be considered" (162). Hernández also says that "Chicana/o queer perspectives and intellectual thought disclose hegemonic cultural reliance on gender surveillance and on the manipulation of desires" (156).

13. For a discussion of jotería studies, see Michael Hames-García's "Jotería Studies, or the Political Is Personal," an introduction to a special dossier on the topic in *Aztlán: The Journal of Chicano Studies*. Hames-García says that the definition of jotería is "not fixed," and the dossier's contributors "use it primarily to describe a group of people of Chicana/o or Mexicana/o descent whose lives include dissident practices of gender and sexuality" (139). Hames-García goes on to say that "[t]he extent to which jotería as an identity category, cultural practice, or social process remains distinct from other categories of sexual or gender dissent or nonconformity is an open question to be debated within jotería studies" (139). A critical jotería studies remains attentive to questions of gender variance in jotería contexts.

14. Licia Fiol-Matta states that "[e]fforts to queer the word 'queer' from Spanish have resulted in a number of new signifiers such as quiar and cuir. These signifiers have not, to date, replaced the continental and hemispheric use of queer as a shorthand for identities and practices that contest regulatory interpellations" ("Queer/Sexualities" 219).

15. In some of her other writings, Anzaldúa refers to herself as a "half-and-half" or "mita' y mita" (short for mitad y mitad), citing it as a term that "queer women are called in South Texas" (*The Gloria Anzaldúa Reader* 141). I discuss her use of this term in the conclusion.

16. When referring to specific people, I use "Chicana" if the author has been identified as such, and I try to use people's preferred terms if known. Several quotes from secondary materials use "Chicana/o," "Chican@," and other variations. One of the challenges of adopting the "x" strategy arises in its usage in everyday speech, particularly given that the usage is not yet widely known. I have heard various pronunciations, with the most common being "Lah-teen-EX," as though one is going to say "Latino" but changes the final syllable. Another pronunciation is "Latin-ex," and another is "Lah-teen-equis," using the Spanish pronunciation of the letter "x" in the final syllable. The "x" as used in "Latinx," while it may grow more accessible or more familiar to lay readers over time, can cause greater confusion when used in some other words. For example, the word "todos" (all) and its variations, such as the feminine "todas" and the combined forms "todas/os" and "tod@s," can become unwieldy when the "x" enters the picture. Pronouncing "todxs" can be daunting for the unfamiliar, perhaps particularly monolingual English speakers. For some, the confusion may become a desired disruption that causes people to contemplate the "x" and reconsider the hegemony of the binary as it operates on the construction of language and ideologies. Perhaps over time, what may emerge is a more phonetic spelling such as "Latinex" or "Latinequis." The newly constructed terminology has emerged at a time when it has become even more crucial for the United States to more broadly accept that todxs Chicanxs and Latinxs are indeed an integral part of its population. While some readers may at first resist such hybrid neologisms, the terms "Chicanx" and "Latinx" have nonetheless begun to circulate in activist and literary communities.

17. Adelina Anthony's recent film *Bruising for Besos,* which explores dating violence, is set primarily in L.A. but mentions several Texas cities. I discuss *Bruising for Besos* in chapter 1.

18. In the introduction to the "Trans-" special issue of *Women's Studies Quarterly* (2008), Susan Stryker, Paisley Currah, and Lisa Jean Moore state that "'[t]ransing,' in short, is a practice that takes place within, as well as across or between, gendered spaces. It is a practice that assembles gender into contingent structures of association with other attributes of bodily being, and that allows for their reassembly" (13).

19. In the section titled "Traitor Begets Traitor," Moraga says that "[w]hat I wanted from my mother was impossible. It would have meant her going

against Mexican/Chicano tradition in a very fundamental way. You are a traitor to your race if you do not put the man first. The potential accusation of 'traitor' or 'vendida' is what hangs over the heads and beats in the hearts of most Chicanas seeking to develop our own autonomous sense of ourselves, particularly through sexuality" (103).

20. In his keyword article "Translatinas/os," Lawrence La Fountain-Stokes describes marimacha as referring to a "masculine woman, lesbian, butch" (238). Some also use the term to refer to an assertive or bold woman.

21. Arrizón further points out that the work of destabilizing gender here is an endeavor of borderlands space: "In its hyphenated form, mari-macha may represent a version of 'queer' interpolation, suggesting a genealogy where the 'feminine' and 'masculine' come together—a location where gender is fluid and destabilized" (*Queering Mestizaje* 162). Arrizón goes on to say that "[t]he masculinization of the brown female body requires the 'liminal' negotiation of cultural difference" (162).

22. Emphasis in the original.

23. According to Lourdes Torres in the introduction to the 2003 coedited anthology *Tortilleras: Hispanic & U.S. Latina Lesbian Expression*, terms such as "marimacho," "tortillera," and "jota" have been reclaimed: "Although these words are often used in derogatory ways, Hispanic and Latina lesbians have reappropriated many of them as affirming identity markers" (6).

1. Chicana Masculinities

1. Bergman says that "butches are monosyllabic, until you get to know them, which they will not allow but want, or will allow and want, or will allow but don't want, or won't allow and don't want, so you may or may not get to know them, but you should try, or not" (*Butch Is a Noun*, 15–16).

2. For a discussion on the relation between mestizaje and queer, see Alicia Arrizón's book *Queer Mestizaje* in which she posits that "the 'queering' of mestizaje and the 'mestiza-ing' of the queer as academic/geographic/ intellectual contact zones help to underscore how the negotiations of transcultural postcolonial sites are implicated within contestatory 'acts' or representation" (15). For discussions on the problematic racial logics of mestizaje, see Juliet Hooker's "Hybrid Subjectivities, Latin American

Mestizaje, and Latino Political Thought on Race," María Josefina Saldaña-Portillo's *The Revolutionary Imagination in the Americas and the Age of Development,* and Taunya Lovell Banks's *"Mestizaje* and the Mexican *Mestizo* Self: *No Hay Sangre Negra,* So There Is No Blackness."

3. Keynote Address, University of Texas at Austin, Latino Leadership Council, October 2009.

4. For a discussion of the rasquache as a working-class form of art and survival, see Tomás Ybarra Frausto's "Rasquachismo: A Chicano Sensibility" in *Chicano Art: Resistance and Affirmation, 1965–1985,* edited by Richard Griswold del Castillo, Teresa McKenna, and Yvonne Yarbro-Bejarano (Los Angeles: Wight Art Gallery, UCLA, 1991). Ybarra Frausto locates the rasquache aesthetic as a form of Mexican American vernacular expression, emphasizing the use of common objects and resources to express an attitude of cultural strength and survival. Amalia Mesa-Bains critiques Ybarra Frausto's definition of what constitutes the rasquache, citing it as unnecessarily masculinist. She looks to the "domestic" in order consider feminine forms of rasquachismo. However, because Mesa-Bains offers only women artists as examples of those who can contribute to this feminine domestic form of rasquachismo, I contend that her definition is limiting as well, failing to take into account artists who queer the concept of rasquachismo as a gendered practice.

5. For an in-depth analysis of the contested notion of home for queer Chicanas, see Marivel T. Danielson's *Homecoming Queers: Desire and Difference in Chicana Latina Cultural Production.*

6. We can see this as well in nonbutch-identified characters expressing Chicana masculinities. For example, in Virginia Grise's award-winning play *Blu,* the character Hailstorm models alternative nurturing forms of masculinity and femininity for her partner's children as they navigate the sometimes brutal landscape of gender in a Chicanx community under duress.

2. Ambiguous Chicanx Bodies

1. The National New Play Network and Borderlands Theater commissioned a theatrical adaptation of Viramontes's *Their Dogs Came with Them,* to be adapted by award-winning playwright Virginia Grise.

2. In an interview conducted by Daniel Olivas for La Bloga, Viramontes describes her own experience seeing bulldozers demolish neighborhoods in her beloved East L.A.: "The bulldozers resembled the conqueror's ships coming to colonize a second time and I felt a desire to portray the lives of those who disappeared" (n.p.).

3. For an analysis of the term "manflora" see Marivel T. Danielson's *Homecoming Queers*, which discusses the word's usage by writers Gloria Anzaldúa, Cherríe Moraga, and Lidia Tirado White (28).

4. Viego says that "the repeated themes of wholeness, completeness, and transparency with respect to ethnic-racialized subjectivity are what provide racist discourse with precisely the notion of subjectivity that it needs in order to function most effectively" (4).

5. For more on Arizona's notorious ethnic studies ban, see Belinda Acosta's March 13, 2012, article in the *Texas Observer* on the ban and the Librotraficante movement that writers such as Tony Díaz have mobilized in response. See also the Librotraficante website at http://www.librotraficante.com/.

3. Transing Chicanidad

1. For more on Nahuatl poetics, see Karl Taube, Miguel Léon-Portilla, and Rafael Pérez-Torres.

2. See also Laura Pérez for a discussion of the diphrasm or difrasismo, "a unique Nahua literary trope that invokes a third element through the yoking of two others" (14). Pérez says that "[u]ltimately, as a poetic figure of speech, reflecting a frame of mind attempting to balance differences, the diphrasm conveys the insufficiency of signifying systems, whether alphabetical, hieroglyphic, or pictographic, to fully capture meaning, not least when what is referred to is of an especially unknowable nature to humans, such as spirituality and the divine, or unknowable because unfamiliar to us, as in cultural difference" (14).

3. For analyses of queer Chicano cultural production and the tensions between queerness and notions of "family," see Richard T. Rodríguez's *Next of Kin: The Family in Chicano/a Cultural Politics* and Rita Urquijo-Ruiz's *Wild Tongues: Transnational Mexican Popular Culture*. For a consideration of such queer familial tensions and dynamics in the context

of war and militarization, see Ariana Vigil's *War Echoes: Gender and Militarization in U.S. Latina/o Cultural Production.*

4. In teaching this novel, I have had several trans students remark that they appreciate the representation of Frank and the fact that the novel is not a coming-out novel or about Frank's transition but instead it is about aspects of Frank's life and relationships.

5. For a discussion of disability in *Like Son,* see Julie Avril Minich's *Accessible Citizenships.* For an analysis of queerness and disability, see Alison Kafer's *Feminist, Queer, Crip.*

6. In the public talk "Discussion of Lost Son" on a panel titled "Writing from an International Persective," Lemus describes this novel as an immigrant novel.

7. For a provocative discussion of "various spatial practices of resistance and survival" (79), see *On Making Sense: Queer Race Narratives of Intelligibility* by Ernesto Javier Martínez.

8. In her examination of Coyolxauhqui, Alicia Gaspar de Alba says that "Coyolxuahqui was framed" and requires an "unframing" so that we can imagine more complex and just versions of the myth (*[Un]Framing the "Bad Woman"* 192). She goes on to write an alternate version of the story.

9. Anzaldúa evokes Coyolxauhqui in her work, such as in her discussion of Chicana feminist creative processes as a breaking open and remaking in her 1999 "Putting Coyolxauhqui Together: A Creative Process." Coyolxauhqui can help us think about the creative reconfigurations performed by gender variant Chicanx poste-borderlands subjects. For an analysis of the role of Coyolxauhqui and other indigenous goddesses in Anzladúa's work, see Theresa Delgadillo's *Spiritual Mestizaje.*

4. Brokeback Rancho

1. The chapter's title is indebted to Adelina Anthony's quip in her show *La Angry Xicana?!* that a queer Chicana version of "Brokeback Mountain" would be called "Brokeback Rancho."

2. For another interesting example of a recovered Mexican American text, see Amelia María de la Luz Montes's critical introduction to Maria Amparo Ruiz de Burton's *Who Would Have Thought It?*

3. For analyses of queerness and sexuality in relation to the historical romance genre, see Lisa Lynne Moore's "Acts of Union: Sexuality and Nationalism, Romance and Realism in the Irish National Tale" and Alexandra Barron's "Fantasies of Union: The Queer National Romance in *My Beautiful Laundrette.*"

4. B. V. Olguín, in "*Caballeros* and Indians," describes the character of Luis as a "cryptically queer son" (37) and a "possibly queer son" (39). Olguín argues that "González and Eimer actually reinforce racist tropes against mestiza/os and Indians in the guise of challenging the neo-feudal socio-economic order that gave rise to these tropes" (39).

5. González is writing this after the Mexican Revolution and World War I and in a region that continues to be highly segregated along Mexican and Anglo lines. Much of the novel's content is inflected by her anthropological research in areas of South Texas that continue to be predominantly populated by people of Mexican descent.

6. In fact, one may even say that the collaborators form treaties—the Treaty of Guadalupe Hidalgo between Mexico and the United States was negotiated and signed in 1848 by Luis Gonzaga Cuevas (no known relation). Given González's background as a researcher and her familiarity with the period, it is unlikely that the namesake is a coincidence.

7. E. E. Mireles and Jovita González Mireles Papers, Collection 44, Box 55, Special Collections and Archives, Mary and Jeff Bell Library, Texas A&M University–Corpus Christi.

8. Several letters from Margaret Eimer to Jovita González begin with the salutation "My Jovita." One that is addressed to "Jovita luv" says "I remember you. I remember the yard with the great trees and the benches where we laughed and spun golden cloth from the threads of our dreams. I remember that we were happy, you and me." Letter dated Dec. 21 (no year) from Margaret Eimer to Jovita González, E. E. Mireles and Jovita González Mireles Papers, Collection 44, Box 1, Special Collections and Archives, Mary and Jeff Bell Library, Texas A&M University–Corpus Christi.

Conclusion

1. For an analysis of the queer Cuban hip-hop duo Las Krudas Cubensi, see Celiany Rivera-Velázquez's film *Reina de mi misma/Queen of Myself:*

Las Krudas d' Cuba as well as Jafari S. Allen's book *¡Venceremos? The Erotics of Black Self-Making in Cuba.*

2. This community would join together again the following summer at Austin's Pride Parade, leading a mobile ritual of mourning for the black and Latinx queer people killed at the Pulse nightclub in Orlando on June 12, 2016.

3. For analyses of Anzaldúa's archive, see *The Gloria Anzaldúa Reader,* edited by AnaLouise Keating, and Suzanne Bost's "Messy Archives and Materials That Matter."

4. For an iconic discussion of women's reclamation of the erotic as a form of power, see Audre Lorde's "The Uses of the Erotic: The Erotic as Power" in *Sister Outsider.* Anzaldúa's exploration of the erotic in her unpublished works aligns here with Lorde's thinking.

5. Special thanks to AnaLouise Keating for talking to me about Anzaldúa's "Heche" story.

6. Sebastián José Colón-Otero stressed this in his talk titled "'I Am More Than Half & Half: A Mita' y Mita' Speaks'; Conocimiento, Secreto, Coatlicue State and Nepantla in My Experience as a Transgender Person of Color," presented at the 2010 conference of the Society for the Study of Gloria Anzaldúa.

7. In *Second Skins,* Jay Prosser mentions Anzaldúa, in particular her "memory of the mita' y mita' figure in the sexual, gender, and geographic borderlands," as an example when claiming that "[t]he transgendered presence lies just below the surface of most lesbian and gay studies' foundational texts" (23).

8. Julia Serano says that trans feminism "extends [a] feminist analysis to transgender issues" ("Trans Feminism" n.p.).

9. For other productive and insightful engagements with trans Latinx studies and theories, see Marcia Ochoa's *Queen for a Day,* Lawrence LaFountain-Stokes' "Translatinas/os," Bamby Salcedo's political organizing work with the TransLatin@ Coalition and other groups (see http://bambysalcedo.com), and Eddy Alvarez's "Finding Sequins in the Rubble."

10. See Crenshaw's "Demarginalizing the Intersection of Race and Sex" and "Mapping the Margins."

11. For a discussion of the influence of black feminist thought on Moraga's work, see the introduction of María C. González's *Contemporary Mexican-American Women Novelists*.

12. This is reminiscent of and has implications for ongoing debates in queer of color theory that call attention to the pitfalls of queer theory's "'subjectless' queer critique" (Hames-García, "Queer Theory Revisited" 39). For more in this discussion, see also Hiram Pérez's *A Taste for Brown Bodies: Gay Modernity and Cosmopolitan Desire*.

13. "Toward a Decolonial Feminism" follows up on Lugones's thinking in her earlier work in "Heterosexualism and the Colonial/Modern Gender System." In this later essay, Lugones remarks that with the earlier article she "did not mean to add a gendered reading and a racial reading to the already understood colonial relations" but instead argues for "a rereading of modern capitalist modernity itself" (742). She goes on to say that "[i]n thinking of the methodology of decoloniality, I move to read the social from the cosmologies that inform it, rather than beginning with a gendered reading of cosmologies informing and constituting perception, motility, embodiment, and relation. Thus the move I am recommending is very different from one that reads gender into the social. The shift can enable us to understand the organization of the social in terms that unveil the deep disruption of the gender imposition in the self in relation." While this move takes us further toward decolonizing gender, Lugones could go further in this later article to explain how heterosexualism informs the cosmologies themselves. She does consider the category of intersexuality as one that productively destabilizes the sex and gender binaries.

14. In considering Lugones's fractured locus, I am reminded of Sheila Marie Contreras's reading of the role that Anzaldúa's image of the crossroads from *Borderlands/La Frontera* has played for Judith Butler. Contreras says that "Anzaldúa provides for Butler the elaboration of a space in which those who are not recognized within the 'legitimate' constructions of subjectivity—culture, nation, race, sexuality—resist immobilization and are instead prompted to redefine the very limits of subjectivity as they negotiate the discursive traffic traveling through the 'crossroads' of consciousness" (115).

15. In considering the claim to "actual innocence," the opinion several times mentions a clinician's psychosexual assessment of the women who found that they "did not fit the profile for sex offenders" (Court of Criminal Appeals of Texas 6) and that "they had never engaged in deviant sexual behavior" (36). The women were convicted and imprisoned in 1997 and 1998. Prior to the passage of *Lawrence v. Texas* (2003) in which the U.S. Supreme Court overturned the Texas antisodomy law, the court might not have been as equipped to do the right thing in this new trial. The road to exoneration was indeed a long one for the San Antonio Four, and changes in the legal code as well as the mainstreaming of queer culture likely helped pave the way for the exoneration. The members of the San Antonio Four also participated in many interviews, fund-raisers, and public talks to raise wider awareness of their cause to obtain the exoneration that they rightly deserved.

Bibliography

Acosta, Belinda. "Librotraficante." *Texas Observer,* March 13, 2012, https://www.texasobserver.org/librotraficante/.

Ahmed, Sara. *Queer Phenomenology: Orientations, Objects, Others.* Durham, NC: Duke University Press, 2006.

Alarcón, Norma. "Making 'Familia' from Scratch: Split Subjectivies in the Work of Helena María Viramontes and Cherríe Moraga." *Chicana Creativity and Criticism: New Frontiers in American Literature.* Ed. María Herrera-Sobek and Helena María Viramontes. Albuquerque: University of New Mexico Press, 1996. 220–32.

———. "The Theoretical Subject(s) of *This Bridge Called My Back* and Anglo-American Feminism." *Making Face, Making Soul/Haciendo Caras: Creative and Critical Perspectives by Feminists of Color.* Ed. Gloria E. Anzaldúa. San Francisco: Aunt Lute Books, 1990. 356–369.

Allen, Jafari S. *¡Venceremos? The Erotics of Black Self-Making in Cuba.* Durham, NC: Duke University Press, 2011.

Alvarez, Eddy Francisco. "Finding Sequins in the Rubble: Stitching Together an Archive of Trans Latina Los Angeles." *TSQ: Transgender Studies Quarterly* 3.3–4 (2016): 618–27.

Anthony, Adelina, dir. *Bruising for Besos.* Prod. Adelina Anthony and Marisa Becerra. AdeRisa Productions, 2016.

———. *Bruising for Besos* [website]. 2017, http://www.bruisingforbesos.com/synopsis/4578238645.

———. "Introduction: Bruising for Besos." *Chicana/Latina Studies* 9.2 (Spring 2010): 62–95.

———. "Mastering Sex and Tortillas." Unpublished play, 2009.

Anzaldúa, Gloria. *Borderlands/La Frontera: The New Mestiza.* San Francisco: Aunt Lute Books, 1987.

———. Gloria Evangelina Anzaldúa Papers, 1942–2004. Nettie Lee Benson Latin American Collection, University of Texas, Austin.

———. *The Gloria Anzaldúa Reader.* Ed. AnaLouise Keating. Durham, NC: Duke University Press, 2009.

———. *Interviews/Entrevistas.* Ed. AnaLouise Keating. New York: Routledge, 2000.

———, ed. *Making Face, Making Soul/Haciendo Caras: Creative and Critical Perspectives by Feminists of Color.* San Francisco: Aunt Lute Books, 1990.

———. "Putting Coyolxauhqui Together: A Creative Process." *How We Work.* Ed. Marla Morris, Mary Aswell Doll, and William E. Pinar. Peter Lang, 1999.

———. "To(o) Queer the Writer—*Loca, escritora y chicana.*" *Living Chicana Theory.* Ed. Carla Trujillo. Berkeley: Third Woman, 1998.

Arrizón, Alicia. *Latina Performance: Traversing the Stage.* Bloomington: Indiana University Press, 1999.

———. *Queering Mestizaje: Transculturation and Performance.* Ann Arbor: University of Michigan Press, 2006.

Arteaga, Alfred. *Chicano Poetics: Heterotexts and Hybridities.* Cambridge: Cambridge University Press, 1997.

Aultman, B. "Cisgender." Ed. Paisley Currah and Susan Stryker. *Transgender Studies Quarterly* 1.1–2 (2014): 61–62.

Bamby Salcedo. 2017, http://bambysalcedo.com.

Banks, Taunya Lovell. "*Mestizaje* and the Mexican *Mestizo* Self: *No Hay Sangre Negra,* So There Is No Blackness." *Latino/a Condition.* Ed. Richard Delgado and Jean Stefancic. 2nd ed. New York: New York University Press, 2010. 463–66.

Barajas, Michael. "Freeing the San Antonio Four." *San Antonio Current,* November 13, 2012, www.sacurrent.com/sanantonio/freeing-the-san -antonio-four/Content?oid=2245220.

Barron, Alexandra. "Fantasies of Union: The Queer National Romance in My Beautiful Laundrette." *Genders* 45 (2007).

Bebout, Lee. "The First Last Generation: Queer Temporality, Heteropatriarchy, and Cultural Reproduction in Jovita González and Eve Raleigh's Caballero." *Western American Literature* 49.4 (2015): 351–74.

Bergman, S. Bear. *Butch Is a Noun.* San Francisco: Suspect Thoughts, 2006.

Berlant, Lauren, and Michael Warner. "Sex in Public." *Critical Inquiry* 24.2 (Winter 1998): 547–66.

Bost, Suzanne. "Messy Archives and Materials That Matter: Making Knowledge with the Gloria E. Anzaldúa Papers." *PMLA* 130.2 (2015): 615–30.

———. "Unsafe Politics and Risky Connections." *Journal of the Midwest Modern Language Association* 46.2 (2013): 127–40.

Brady, Mary Pat. "Metaphors to Love By: Toward a Chicana Aesthetics in Their Dogs Came with Them." *Rebozos de Palabras: An Helena María Viramontes Critical Reader.* Ed. Gabriella Gutierrez y Muhs. Tucson: University of Arizona Press, 2013. 167–91.

Brooks, Joanna. "Working Definitions: Race, Ethnic Studies, and Early American Literature." *Early American Literature* 41.2 (2006): 313–20.

Bryant, Tisa. *Unexplained Presence.* Providence, RI: Leon Works, 2007.

Burana, Lily, and Roxxie Linnea Due, eds. *Dagger: On Butch Women.* Pittsburgh: Cleis, 1994.

Butler, Judith. *Gender Trouble: Feminism and the Subversion of Identity.* 10th anniversary ed. New York: Routledge, 2006.

Butterworth, Lisa. "Black Lives Matter Co-Founder Patrisse Cullors on Intersectionality in Activism." *BUST Magazine,* n.d., https://bust.com /feminism/19122-the-making-of-a-movement-q-a-with-patrisse-cullors -of-blm.html.

Calvo, Luz, and Catrióna Rueda Esquibel. "Our Queer Kin." *Gay Latino Studies: A Critical Reader.* Ed. Michael Hames-García and Ernesto Javier Martínez. Durham, NC: Duke University Press, 2011. 105–12.

Chammah, Maurice. "The Mystery of the San Antonio Four." *Texas Observer,* January 7, 2014, http://www.texasobserver.org/mystery-san -antonio-four/.

Colón-Otero, Sebastián José. "'I Am More Than Half & Half: A Mita' Y Mita' Speaks'; Conocimiento, Secreto, Coatlicue State and Nepantla in My Experience as a Transgender Person of Color." *El Munzo Zurdo: Conference of the Society for the Study of Gloria Anzaldúa,* 2010.

Contreras, Sheila Marie. *Blood Lines: Myth, Indigenism, and Chicana/o Literature.* Austin: University of Texas Press, 2009.

Cotera, María Eugenia. "Introduction: A Woman of the Borderlands." *Life along the Border: A Landmark Tejana Thesis, by Jovita González.* Ed.

María Eugenia Cotera. College Station: Texas A&M University Press, 2006. 3–33.

———. *Native Speakers: Ella Deloria, Zora Neale Hurston, Jovita González, and the Poetics of Culture.* Austin: University of Texas Press, 2008.

Court of Criminal Appeals of Texas. "Ex Parte Mayhugh [N1] NOS. WR-84,700–01 & WR-84,700–02." November 23, 2016, http://www.search.txcourts.gov.

Crenshaw, Kimberlé. "Demarginalizing the Intersection of Race and Sex: A Black Feminist Critique of Antidiscrimination Doctrine, Feminist Theory, and Antiracist Politics." *University of Chicago Legal Forum* 1 (1989): 139–67.

———. "Mapping the Margins: Intersectionality, Identity Politics, and Violence against Women of Color." *Stanford Law Review* 43.6 (1991): 1241–99.

Curl, John. "Ancient American Poets: The Flower Songs of Nezahualcoyotl." *Bilingual Review/La Revista Bilingüe* 26.2 (2001): 1–45.

Cvetkovich, Ann. "Untouchability and Vulnerability: Stone Butchness as Emotional Style." *Butch/Femme: Inside Lesbian Gender.* Ed. Sally R. Munt. London: Cassell, 1998. 159–69.

Danielson, Marivel T. *Homecoming Queers: Desire and Difference in Chicana Latina Cultural Production.* New Brunswick, NJ: Rutgers University Press, 2009.

Delgadillo, Theresa. *Spiritual Mestizaje: Religion, Gender, Race, and Nation in Contemporary Chicana Narrative.* Durham, NC: Duke University Press, 2011.

Enke, A. Finn. *Transfeminist Perspectives in and beyond Transgender and Gender Studies.* Philadelphia: Temple University Press, 2012.

Esquenazi, Deborah S. *Southwest of Salem.* 2016, http://www.southwestofsalem.com/.

———, dir. *Southwest of Salem: The Story of the San Antonio Four.* FilmRise, 2017.

Esquibel, Catrióna Rueda. *With Her Machete in Her Hand: Reading Chicana Lesbians.* Austin: University of Texas Press, 2006.

Faderman, Lillian. "The Return of Butch and Femme: A Phenomenon in Lesbian Sexuality of the 1980s and 1990s." *Journal of the History of Sexuality* 2 (1992): 578–96.

Feinberg, Leslie. *Trans Liberation.* Boston: Beacon, 1999.

Ferguson, Roderick A. *Aberrations in Black: Toward a Queer of Color Critique.* Minneapolis: University of Minnesota Press, 2004.

Fiol-Matta, Licia. "Queer/Sexualities." *Critical Terms in Caribbean and Latin American Thought: Historical and Institutional Trajectories.* Ed. Yolanda Martínez-San Miguel, Ben Sifuentes-Jáuregui, and Marisa Belausteguigoitia. New York: Palgrave Macmillan, 2016. 217–30.

Foxx, Dino. "Xicana Artist Adelina Anthony on the Evolution of Bruising for Besos." *Out in SA,* July 5, 2016, http://outinsa.com/xicana-artist -adelina-anthony-on-the-evolution-of-bruising-for-besos/.

Galarte, Francisco. "On Trans* Chican@s: Amor, Justicia, y Dignidad." *Aztlán: A Journal of Chicano Studies* 39.1 (2014): 229–36.

Gámez, Rocky. "From *The Gloria Stories.*" *The Persistent Desire.* Ed. Joan Nestle. Boston: Alyson Books, 1992. 202–07.

Garza-Falcón, Leticia M. *Gente Decente: A Borderlands Response to the Rhetoric of Dominance.* Austin: University of Texas Press, 1998.

Gaspar de Alba, Alicia. *Desert Blood: The Juárez Murders.* Houston: Arte Público, 2005.

———. "Thirty Years of Chicana/Latina Lesbian Literary Production." *The Routledge Companion to Latino/a Literature.* Ed. Suzanne Bost and Frances R. Aparicio. Hoboken: Taylor and Francis, 2012. 462–75.

———. *[Un]Framing the "Bad Woman": Sor Juana, Malinche, Coyolxauhqui, and Other Rebels with a Cause.* Austin: University of Texas Press, 2014.

Gilmore, Ruth Wilson. "Race and Globalization." *Geographies of Global Change: Remapping the World.* Ed. R. J. Johnston, Peter J. Taylor, and Michael Watts. 2nd ed. Malden, MA: Wiley-Blackwell, 2002. 261–74.

Gómez-Barris, Macarena, and Licia Fiol-Matta. "Introduction: Las Américas Quarterly." *American Quarterly* 66.3 (2014): 493–504.

González, Jovita. *Dew on the Thorn.* Houston, TX: Arte Público, 1997.

González, Jovita, and Eve Raleigh [pseud. for Margaret Eimer]. *Caballero: A Historical Novel.* Ed. José E. Limón and María Cotera. College Station: Texas A&M University Press, 1996.

———. E. E. Mireles and Jovita González Mireles Papers. Special Collections and Archives, Mary and Jeff Bell Library, Texas A&M University, Corpus Christi.

González, María C. *Contemporary Mexican-American Women Novelists: Toward a Feminist Identity.* New York: Peter Lang, 1998.

Graff, E. J. "My Trans Problem." *The Village Voice*, June 19, 2001, http://www
.villagevoice.com/2001/06/19/my-trans-problem/.

Grise, Virginia. *Blu*. New Haven, CT: Yale University Press, 2011.

Gutiérrez, Raquel. "The Barber of East L.A." Unpublished play, 2009.

———. *Butchlalis de Panochtitlan*. 2013, https://myspace.com/butchlalis.

Gutiérrez y Muhs, Gabriella, ed. *Rebozos de Palabras: An Helena María Viramontes Critical Reader*. Tucson: University of Arizona Press, 2013.

Halberstam, J. Jack. *Female Masculinity*. Durham, NC: Duke University
Press, 1998.

———. *In a Queer Time and Place: Transgender Bodies, Subcultural Lives*.
New York: New York University Press, 2005.

Halberstam, J. Jack, and Del LaGrace Volcano. *The Drag King Book*. London:
Serpent's Tail, 1999.

Hames-García, Michael. "Jotería Studies, or the Political Is Personal."
Aztlán: A Journal of Chicano Studies 39.1 (2014): 135–42.

———. "Queer Theory Revisited." *Gay Latino Studies: A Critical Reader*. Ed.
Michael Hames-García and Ernesto Javier Martínez. Durham, NC:
Duke University Press, 2011. 19–45.

Hernández, Ellie. *Postnationalism in Chicana/o Literature and Culture*. Austin: University of Texas Press, 2010.

Hooker, Juliet. "Hybrid Subjectivities, Latin American Mestizaje, and
Latin Political Thought on Race." *Politics, Groups, and Identities* 2.2
(2014): 188–201.

Hsu, Hsuan L. "Fatal Contiguities: Metonymy and Environmental Justice."
New Literary History 42.1 (2011): 147–68.

Indigenous Environmental Network. "#NoDAPL Last Stand Call to
Action!: Dept. of Army Approves DAPL Easement." http://www
.ienearth.org/nodapl-last-stand-call-to-action/.

Jackson, Claire M. "About Claire de Lunacy." *Claire De Lunacy*, n.d., http://
wildgender.com/queering-short-fiction-camille-by-claire-m-jackson/2630.

———. "Camille." *Wild Gender*, May 29, 2012.

Kafer, Alison. *Feminist, Queer, Crip*. Bloomington: Indiana University Press,
2013.

Kennedy, Elizabeth Lapovsky, and Madeline D. Davis. *Boots of Leather, Slippers of Gold: The History of a Lesbian Community*. New York: Routledge,
1993.

Kevane, Bridget A. *Profane & Sacred: Latino/a American Writers Reveal the Interplay of the Secular and the Religious.* Lanham, MD: Rowman & Littlefield, 2008.

La Fountain-Stokes, Lawrence. "Translatinas/Os." *TSQ: Transgender Studies Quarterly* 1.1–2 (2014): 237–41.

Lemus, Felicia Luna. "Discussion of Like Son." *C-SPAN*, October 8, 2013, https://www.c-span.org/video/?c4467869/felicia-luna-lemus.

———. *Like Son: A Novel.* New York: Akashic Books, 2007.

———. *Trace Elements of Random Tea Parties.* Berkeley, CA: Seal, 2003.

Léon-Portilla, Miguel. *Fifteen Poets of the Aztec World.* Norman: University of Oklahoma Press, 2000.

Librotraficante. 2016, http://www.librotraficante.com/.

Leyva, Yolanda Chávez. "Gloria Anzaldúa's Legacy Will Continue to Inspire Generations." *The Progressive*, June 9, 2004, http://progressive.org/op-eds/gloria-anzaldua-s-legacy-will-continue-inspire-generations/.

Lima, Lázaro. *The Latino Body: Crisis Identities in American Literary and Cultural Memory.* New York: New York University Press, 2007.

Limón, José E. "Introduction." *Caballero: A Historical Novel.* Eds. José E. Limón and María Cotera. College Station: Texas A&M University Press, 1996. xii–xxvi.

López-Calvo, Ignacio. *Latino Los Angeles in Film and Fiction: The Cultural Production of Social Anxiety.* Tucson: University of Arizona Press, 2011.

Lorde, Audre. *Sister Outsider: Essays and Speeches.* Trumansburg, NY: Crossing Press, 1984.

Lugones, Maria. "Heterosexualism and the Colonial/Modern Gender System." *Hypatia* 22.1 (2007): 186–209.

———. "Toward a Decolonial Feminism." *Hypatia* 25.4 (2010): 742–59.

Luibhéid, Eithne, and Lionel Cantú Jr., eds. *Queer Migrations: Sexuality, U.S. Citizenship, and Border Crossings.* Minneapolis: University of Minnesota Press, 2005.

Martin, Del, and Phyllis Lyon. *Lesbian/Woman.* 20th ed. Volcano, CA: Volcano Press, 1991.

Martín Alcoff, Linda. "The Unassimilated Theorist." *The History of the Book and the Idea of Literature.* Special issue of *PMLA* 121.1 (2006): 255–59.

Martínez, Ernesto. *On Making Sense: Queer Race Narratives of Intelligibility.* Stanford, CA: Stanford University Press, 2012.

May, Vivian M. *Pursuing Intersectionality, Unsettling Dominant Imaginaries.* New York: Routledge, 2015.

Mendoza, Elvia. "States of Dismemberment: State Violence and the Un/Making of Queer Subjectivities." Dissertation, University of Texas, Austin, 2016.

Mermann-Jozwiak, Elisabeth, and Nancy Sullivan. *Conversations with Mexican American Writers: Languages and Literatures in the Borderlands.* Jackson: University Press of Mississippi, 2009.

Mesa-Bains, Amalia. "'Domesticana': The Sensibility of Chicana Rasquache." *Aztlan* 24.2 (1999): 155–67.

Minich, Julie Avril. *Accessible Citizenships: Disability, Nation, and the Cultural Politics of Greater Mexico.* Philadelphia: Temple University Press, 2013.

Miranda, Deborah A. "Extermination of the Joyas: Gendercide in Spanish California." *GLQ: A Journal of Lesbian and Gay Studies* 16.1–2 (2010): 253–84.

Moore, Lisa L. "Acts of Union: Sexuality and Nationalism, Romance and Realism in the Irish National Tale." *Cultural Critique* 44 (Winter 2000): 113–44.

Moraga, Cherríe. *The Last Generation: Prose and Poetry.* Cambridge, MA: South End, 1993.

———. *Loving in the War Years: Lo Que Nunca Pasó Por Sus Labios.* Boston: South End, 1983.

Moraga, Cherríe, and Gloria Anzaldúa, eds. *This Bridge Called My Back: Writings by Radical Women of Color.* New York: Kitchen Table, Women of Color Press, 1981.

Muñoz, José Esteban. *Cruising Utopia: The Then and There of Queer Futurity.* New York: New York University Press, 2009.

———. *Disidentifications: Queers of Color and the Performance of Politics.* Cultural Studies of the Americas. Minneapolis: University of Minnesota Press, 1999.

———. "Feeling Brown: Ethnicity and Affect in Ricardo Bracho's *The Sweetest Hangover* (and Other STDs)." *Theatre Journal* 52.1 (2000): 67–79.

Munt, Sally R., ed. *Butch/Femme: Inside Lesbian Gender.* London: Cassell, 1998.

Nash, Jennifer C. "Intersectionality and Its Discontents." *American Quarterly* 69.1 (2017): 117–29.

Nestle, Joan, Clare Howell, and Riki Anne Wilchins, eds. *GenderQueer: Voices from beyond the Sexual Binary.* Boston: Alyson Books, 2002.

Ochoa, Marcia. *Queen for a Day: Transformistas, Beauty Queens, and the Performance of Femininity in Venezuela.* Durham, NC: Duke University Press, 2014.

Olguín, B. V. "*Caballeros* and Indians: Mexican American Whiteness, Hegemonic Mestizaje, and Ambivalent Indigeneity in Proto-Chicana/o Autobiographical Discourse, 1858–2008." *MELUS: Multi-Ethnic Literature of the U.S.* 38.1 (2013): 30–49.

Olivas, Daniel A. "La Bloga: Interview With Helena María Viramontes." *La Bloga,* April 2, 2007, http://labloga.blogspot.com/2007/04/interview -with-helena-mara-viramontes.html.

Paredes, Américo. *George Washington Gomez: A Mexicotexan Novel.* Houston: Arte Público, 1990.

Perez, Domino Renee. *There Was a Woman:* La Llorona *from Folklore to Popular Culture.* Austin: University of Texas Press, 2008.

Pérez, Emma. *The Decolonial Imaginary: Writing Chicanas into History.* Bloomington: Indiana University Press, 1999.

———. "The Will to Feel: Decolonial Anzaldúan Methods." El Mundo Zurdo: International Conference on the Life and Work of Gloria E. Anzaldúa, University of Texas at San Antonio, 2016.

Pérez, Hiram. *A Taste for Brown Bodies: Gay Modernity and Cosmopolitan Desire.* New York: New York University Press, 2015.

———. "You Can Have My Brown Body and Eat It, Too!" *Social Text* 23.3–4 (2005): 171–91.

Pérez, Laura. *Chicana Art: The Politics of Spiritual and Aesthetic Altarities.* Durham, NC: Duke University Press, 2007.

Pérez-Torres, Rafael. *Mestizaje: Critical Uses of Race in Chicano Culture.* Minneapolis: University of Minnesota Press, 2006.

Prosser, Jay. *Second Skins: The Body Narratives of Transsexuality.* New York: Columbia University Press, 1998.

Puar, Jasbir K. "Disability." *TSQ: Transgender Studies Quarterly* 1.1–2 (2014): 77–81.

———. *Terrorist Assemblages: Homonationalism in Queer Times.* Durham, NC: Duke University Press, 2007.

Queen, Carol. *Real Live Nude Girl: Chronicles of Sex-Positive Culture.* San Francisco: Cleis, 1997.

Richardson, Matt. *The Queer Limit of Black Memory: Black Lesbian Literature and Irresolution.* Columbus: Ohio State University Press, 2013.

Rivera-Velázquez, Celiany. *Reina de mi misma/Queen of Myself: Las Krudas d' Cuba.* 2012. https://vimeo.com/46777467.

Rodríguez, Juana María. *Queer Latinidad: Identity Practices, Discursive Spaces.* New York: New York University Press, 2003.

Rodríguez, Richard T. *Next of Kin: The Family in Chicano/a Cultural Politics.* Durham, NC: Duke University Press, 2010.

Ruiz de Burton, Maria Amparo. *Who Would Have Thought It?* Ed. Amelia María de La Luz Montes. New York: Penguin, 2009.

Saldaña-Portillo, María Josefina. *Revolutionary Imagination in the Americas and the Age of Development.* Durham, NC: Duke University Press, 2003.

Saldívar-Hull, Sonia. *Feminism on the Border: Chicana Gender Politics and Literature.* Berkeley: University of California Press, 2000.

"The San Antonio Four Are Declared Innocent and Fully Exonerated by the Texas Court of Criminal Appeals!" *Corriente Latina,* November 26, 2016, http://corrientelatina.com/movies-entertainment/san-antonio-four -declared-innocent-fully-exonerated-texas-court-criminal-appeals/.

Sandoval, Chela. *Methodology of the Oppressed.* Minneapolis: University of Minnesota Press, 2000.

Sedgwick, Eve Kosofsky. *Tendencies.* New York: Routledge, 1994.

Serano, Julia. "Trans Feminism: There's No Conundrum about It." Ms. Blog, April 18, 2012m, http://msmagazine.com/blog/2012/04/18/trans -feminism-theres-no-conundrum-about-it/.

Shea, Renee H. "New Frontiers in Fiction: A Profile of Helena María Viramontes." *Poets and Writers Magazine,* June 2007, 36–42.

Soto, Sandra K. *Reading Chican@ Like a Queer: The De-Mastery of Desire.* Austin: University of Texas Press, 2010.

Stein, Arlene. *Shameless: Sexual Dissidence in American Culture.* New York: New York University Press, 2006.

Stryker, Susan, Paisley Currah, and Lisa Jean Moore. "Introduction: Trans-, Trans, or Transgender?" *WSQ: Women's Studies Quarterly,* 36.3 (2008): 11–22.

Suess, Amets, Karine Espineira, and Pam Crego Walters. "Depathologization." Ed. Paisley Currah and Susan Stryker. *Transgender Studies
Quarterly* 1.1–2 (2014): 77–81.

Taube, Karl A. *Aztec and Maya Myths.* Austin: University of Texas Press,
1997.

Tea, Michelle. "Michelle Tea Talks with Felicia Luna Lemus." *The Believer
Book of Writers Talking to Writers.* Ed. Vendela Vida. San Francisco:
Believer Books, 2005. 175–90.

Torres, Lourdes, and Inmaculada Perpetusa-Seva, eds. *Tortilleras: Hispanic &
U.S. Latina Lesbian Expression.* Philadelphia: Temple University Press,
2003.

"The Treaty of Guadalupe Hidalgo (1848)." National Archives, 2016. https://
www.archives.gov/education/lessons/guadalupe-hidalgo.

Trujillo, Carla, ed. *Chicana Lesbians: The Girls Our Mothers Warned Us About.*
Berkeley, CA: Third Woman, 1991.

Urquijo-Ruiz, Rita E. *Wild Tongues: Transnational Mexican Popular Culture.*
Austin: University of Texas Press, 2012.

Viego, Antonio. *Dead Subjects: Toward a Politics of Loss in Latino Studies.*
Durham, NC: Duke University Press, 2007.

Vigil, Ariana E. *War Echoes: Gender and Militarization in U.S. Latina/o Cultural Production.* New Brunswick, NJ: Rutgers University Press, 2014.

Villa, Raúl Homero. *Barrio-Logos: Space and Place in Urban Chicano Literature and Culture.* Austin: University of Texas Press, 2000.

Viramontes, Helena María. *Their Dogs Came with Them: A Novel.* New York:
Atria, 2007.

Warner, Michael. *Fear of a Queer Planet: Queer Politics and Social Theory.*
Minneapolis: University of Minnesota Press, 1993.

Wiegman, Robyn. *Object Lessons.* Durham, NC: Duke University Press, 2012.

Yarbro-Bejarano, Yvonne. "Queer Storytelling and Temporality in Trace
Elements of Random Tea Parties by Felicia Luna Lemus." *Aztlán: A
Journal of Chicano Studies* 38.1 (2013): 73–94.

———. "Sexuality and Chicana/o Studies: Toward a Theoretical Paradigm
for the Twenty-First Century." *Cultural Studies* 13 (1999): 335–45.

———. *The Wounded Heart: Writing on Cherríe Moraga.* Chicana Matters
Series. Austin: University of Texas Press, 2001.

Zavala, Elizabeth. "'San Antonio Four' Exonerated by Texas Court of Criminal Appeals." *San Antonio Express-News,* November 23, 2016.

Zuarino, John. "An Interview with Felicia Luna Lemus." *Bookslut,* June 2017, http://www.bookslut.com/features/2007_06_011231.php.

Index

activism: Chicano movement, 42–45, 57,
122; coming to consciousness, 69–70;
intersectionality, 77–78, 133–134; lack
of access to, 69–70; queer organizing,
122–123
Ahmed, Sara, 52
Alarcón, Norma, 12
allgo (formerly Austin Latina/o Lesbian,
Gay, Bisexual, and Transgender
Organization/ALLGO), 6, 118–119,
142n7, 150n2
Anthony, Adelina: *Bruising for Besos*,
45–47, 46*fig.*; generational identity, 21;
Mastering Sex and Tortillas, 29, 37–45,
38*fig.*; Moraga and, 39; space in, 21
Anzaldúa, Gloria, 124*fig.*; creative
processes, 148n9; critical readings
of, 11, 12, 127–128, 151n14; gender and,
123–128, 143n15; influence of, 6–10, 7*fig.*,
142–143n11; "To(o) Queer the Writer,"
19, 29–30. *See also* borderlands
Arrizón, Alicia, 24, 29, 145n21
assimilation, 28, 56–57, 89–90, 122–123, 133
"@" ending, 19–20
Aztlán, 72–73, 98, 122–123

Barber of East L.A. (Butchlalis de
Panochtitlan), 29, 47–51, 48*fig.*
Becerra, Marisa, 45
Black Lives Matter, 134
borderlands: applications of, 9; binaries,
125–126; Chicana lesbian texts of,

77–78; criticisms of, 11; genderqueer as,
79–83, 89–91, 99; mestiza consciousness, 8–9
*Borderlands/La Frontera: The New Mes-
tiza* (Anzaldúa), 6, 8, 9
butch: as borderlands gender, 33; Chicana, 34, 51–55, 81–83; in communities
of color, 51–52; as disidentification,
33–34; dismissal of, 37; as emotional
style, 31–32, 145n1; language of, 29–30;
neo-butch, 54–55; old-school, 41–42; as
orientation, 52–53, 146n6; performative,
28, 51–52; terms for, 29–31; working
class, 35–37, 52, 54, 55
Butch Is a Noun (Bergman), 33
butch-femme, 45, 51–55, 81–83
Butchlalis de Panochtitlan, 21, 27–29,
47–48, 47–51, 48*fig.*
Butler, Judith, 33–34, 151n14

Caballero (González): colonialism, 100,
105–106; critical readings of, 115–116;
production history, 107–112; queer
readings of, 23–24, 100–103, 112–114
"Camille" (Jackson), 128–130
Cantú, Lionel, 115–116
Cántu, Norma, 8
Chicanxs and Chicanidad: assimilation,
56–57, 89–90, 122–123, 133; Aztlán,
72–73; butch-femme in, 51–55, 81–83;
butchness in, 29–32, 42–45, 51–55; definition, 141n1; disidentification, 11,

Chicanxs and Chicanidad (*continued*)
89–90, 97–98; gender nonconformity
and, 12–14, 17; historical recovery of,
45, 57, 60–61, 76, 100–103; lesbians and,
77; transgender in, 23, 91–99; use of,
19–20, 144n16; working class, 49.
See also Latinx
chingonas, 30–32
cisgender, 142n4
Coatlicue state, 8, 142n8
colonialism: gender systems, 18; gentrification, 48, 53, 147n2; in historical
fiction, 100, 105–106; of South Texas,
100, 105–106; tropes, 130. *See also*
decolonialism
Cotera, María, 101–102, 108–112
Cotera, Martha, 110
Coyolxauhqui, 98, 148nn8–9
Crenshaw, Kimberlé, 131
Cruising Utopia (Muñoz), 5, 14
Cvetkovich, Ann, 31–33

death, 118–122
*The Decolonial Imaginary: Writing Chica-
nas into History* (Pérez), 15
decolonialism: assimilation and,
56–57, 89–90, 122–123, 133; colonial
gender systems, 18; decolonial
imaginary, 15; feminism, 135–136,
151n13; reclamation of language, 39.
See also colonialism
disability, 134–135
disidentification, 10–11, 11–12
displacement: cultural, 78; family, 67–68,
74, 87–89, 95–97; homelessness, 63–65;
transgender and, 87–89, 95–98; urbanization, 58, 61, 63–65, 67, 147n2
The Drag King Book (Halberstam and
Volcano), 51–52
drag kings, 51–52

Eimar, Margaret (pseud. Eve Raleigh),
107–114, 149n6, 149n8
Esquenazi, Deborah S., 2, 24, 136, 138
Esquibel, Catrióna Rueda, 14

Faderman, Lillian, 53, 54–55
family: loss of, 67–68, 74, 87–89, 95–97;
notions of, 16–17
Female Masculinity (Halberstam), 84
femininities: art and, 106; butchness and,
30–33; femme, 52–55, 81–83; icons of, 14
feminism, 23, 37, 77–78, 135–136, 151n13

Galarte, Francisco, 131
Gamez, Rocky, 21, 22, 29, 35–37
García, Mari, 28, 47
gender binary: borderlands theory and,
4–5, 125–126; butch-femme, 45, 51–55,
81–83; gender variant critique and,
16–17; heteronormativity, 18, 141–142n3;
inclusive language, 19–20, 144n16; trans
experiences, 92–93
gender nonconformity, 5–6, 10–11,
12–14, 17. *See also* genderqueerness;
transgender
gender orientation: butchness as, 52–53,
146n6; signifiers of, 87–88, 92–94, 106
gender variant critique: application to
Anzaldúa's work, 123–128; construction
of, 14–18; contemporary writings and,
128–130; language in, 18–20, 24–25; significance of, 25–26, 139; trans analytics
and, 131. *See also* intersectionality
genderqueerness: as borderlands space,
79–83, 89–91; Chicanx identity and,
4–5, 12–14, 143n12; family relationships and, 87–89; language of, 84–86;
visibility, 90–91
gentrification, 48, 53, 147n2
Gómez-Barris, Macarena, 20
González, Jovita: collaboration with
Eimar, 107–114, 149n6, 149n8; critical
readings of, 100–102, 149n4; queer
readings of, 23–24, 103–105; settings,
21, 149n5
Graff, E. J., 5
Gutiérrez, Raquel, 28, 47

Halberstam, Jack, 22, 51–52, 59, 84
"Heche" (Anzaldúa), 123–128, 124*fig.*

heteronormativity, 18, 141–142n3. *See also* gender binary

"Heterosexualism and the Colonial/Modern Gender System" (Lugones), 18

history: place of queer Chicanxs in, 15, 45, 57, 60–61; queer recovery, 100–103; queering of, 14–15, 56–57; South Texas, 101, 107–110, 112, 149n5; transing of, 91–92

identity: Chicanx queerness, 4–5, 12–14, 143n12; loss of, 89–90, 97–98; masculinity, 103; *vs.* orientation, 52–53, 146n6

intersectionality: gender variant critique, 77–78, 99, 131–138; queer readings, 16

intersex, 128

Jackson, Claire M., 24, 128–130

jota, 29

jotería, 18, 143n13

language: of butchness, 29–30; construction of, 50; inclusiveness, 19–20; layering of, 84–86; politics of, 18–19, 143n15, 144n16; racial slurs, 94, 105; reclamation, 25, 39, 47–48, 145n23; use of Nahuatl terms, 19, 30, 39, 46, 84

The Last Generation (Moraga), 122–123

Latina Performance (Arrizón), 29

Latinx, use of, 19–20, 144n16. *See also* Chicanxs/Chicanidad

Lawrence v. Texas, 152n15

Lemus, Felicia Luna, 3; critical readings of, 77–83; disidentification, 10–11; *Like Son,* 9–10

lesbians: in Chicana context, 29–30; influence of Anzaldúa, 6–10, 7*fig.,* 142–143n11

Lesbian/Woman (Martin and Lyon), 37

Like Son (Lemus), 9–10, 91–99

Lima, Lázaro, 72

Limón, José, 101–102, 107–112

Los Angeles, 21, 53, 60–66

loss: of community, 89–90, 97–98; of culture, 122–123; death, 118–122; of family, 67–68, 74, 87–89, 95–97; of home, 58, 63–65, 67, 78, 147n2

Loving in the War Years (Moraga), 30–32

Lugones, María, 18, 135

Lyon, Phyllis, 37

Making Face, Making Soul/Haciendo Caras (Anzaldúa), 6

malflora, 68

marimacha, 24–25, 145n20

Martin, Del, 37

masculinities: Chicano movement, 16; cultural assumptions, 27–28; working class, 96–98. *See also* butch

Mastering Sex and Tortillas (Anthony), 29, 38*fig.*

May, Vivian, 132, 133

Mendoza, Elvia, 3, 137

mestiza consciousness, 8–11, 90, 124

mestizaje, 145–146n2

mita' y mita, 125, 143n15

Moraga, Cherríe: Anthony and, 39; Aztlán, 73, 122; butchness in, 22, 29, 30–32; Chicano movement, 122–123; influence on later generations, 21

Muñoz, José Esteban, 5, 10–12, 14

Nahuatl, 19, 30, 39, 46, 84

Nash, Jennifer C., 132

Native Speakers (Cotera), 108

Next of Kin: The Family in Cultural Politics (Rodríguez, R.), 16–17, 25

Ochoa, Marcia, 28

patlache, 19, 30

Perez, Domino Renee, 20

Pérez, Emma, 15, 135

place: Aztlán, 72–73, 98, 122–123; orientation to, 53; queering of, 21–22, 60–66

police violence, 42–43, 62, 66, 73

political criticism, 42–45, 53

post-borderlands theory: decolonial imaginary and, 15; gender nonconformity and, 10–11; genderqueer and, 89–91, 99; borderlands theory and, 12–14, 143n12. *See also* gender variant critique
potentiality, 14
Puar, Jasbir, 134–135
Pursuing Intersectionality, Unsettling Dominant Imaginaries (May), 133

Queen, Carol, 32, 53
Queer Latinidad (Rodríguez, J.), 18–19
Queer Phenomenology: Orientations, Objects, Others (Ahmed), 52
Queering Mestizaje (Arrizón), 24
queerness: activism, 122–123; approaches to Chicanx texts, 16; contentious history of, 19; death and, 118–122; definitions, 18–19; disidentification and, 10–11; exclusion of Chicanxs, 122–123; gender nonconformity and, 5–6; mestizaje and, 145–146n2; postnationalism, 143n12; as potentiality, 14; queer readings, 23–24, 100–103; racialized, 23, 94, 130; time and place, 21–22, 59–60. *See also* intersectionality

race: colonial gender system, 18; feminism and, 23, 37, 77–78, 135–136, 151n13; loss of identity, 89–90, 97–98; racial slurs, 94, 105; racialized gender, 23, 94, 130; tensions with gender identities, 17, 105
Raleigh, Eve (pseud. of Margaret Eimar), 107–114, 149n6, 149n8
Ramirez, Elizabeth, 1–2, 3
rasquache, 43–45, 146n4
Rivera, Cassandra, 1
Rodríguez, Claudia, 28, 47
Rodríguez, Juana María, 18–19
Rodríguez, Richard T., 16–17, 25

Saldívar-Hull, Sonia, 71–72
San Antonio Four, 1–3, 24, 136*fig.*, 137–138, 137*fig.*, 152n15

sexuality: femininity and, 14; heteronormativity, 18, 141–142n3; racialization, 2, 11, 16, 28, 117; relation to gender, 3–5, 12. *See also* lesbians; queerness
South Texas: allgo, 6, 118–119, 142n7, 150n2; Anzaldúa's influence on, 8; colonialism in, 100, 105–106; histories of, 101, 107–110, 112, 149n5; San Antonio Four, 1–3, 24, 136*fig.*, 137–138, 137*fig.*, 152n15; as setting, 21, 22, 35, 53, 149n5
Southwest of Salem (documentary), 2, 4*fig.*, 24, 136

Texas: allgo, 6, 118–119, 142n7, 150n2; Anzaldúa's influence on, 8; colonialism in, 100, 105–106; histories of, 101, 107–110, 112, 149n5; San Antonio Four, 1–3, 24, 136*fig.*, 137–138, 137*fig.*, 152n15; as setting, 21, 22, 35, 53, 149n5
Their Dogs Came with Them (Viramontes): Chicanx history, 60–61; genre conventions and, 23, 75–76; time in, 57–58; urbanization as colonialism in, 62–63, 66–67, 74, 147n2
"The Theoretical Subject(s) of *This Bridge Called My Back* and Anglo-American Feminism" (Alarcón), 12
This Bridge Called My Back: Writings by Radical Women of Color (Anzaldúa and Moraga), 6, 12
time, 21–22, 56–59, 74
"To(o) Queer the Writer" (Anzaldúa), 19, 29–30
tortillera, 29
"Toward a Decolonial Feminism," 135, 151n13
Trace Elements of Random Tea Parties (Lemus), 3, 84–89
transgender: Anzaldúa's writings on, 123–128; Chicanidad and, 79, 91–99; displacement and, 95–98; subjectivities in, 23; visibility, 90–91. *See also* genderqueerness

"Untouchability and Vulnerability: Stone Butchness as Emotional Style" (Cvetkovich), 31–33

U.S.-Mexico border: Anglo colonization of, 100, 105–106; Chicanxphobia, 42–43, 62–63, 74–75; physical and psychic, 9, 13; queering histories, 23–24; as setting, 21, 22, 35, 53, 149n5

Vasquez, Anna, 1–3

Viramontes, Helena María: critical readings of, 58–59; generational identity, 21; queer in, 59–60

With Her Machete in Her Hand: Reading Chicana Lesbians (Esquibel), 14

working class: butch, 35–37, 52, 54, 55; Chicanx, 49; masculinity, 96–98; rasquache, 146n4

The Wounded Heart: Writing on Cherríe Moraga (Yarbro-Bejarano), 15–16

"x" ending, 19–20, 144n16

Xiqana, 39

Yarbro-Bejarano, Yvonne: *The Wounded Heart: Writing on Cherríe Moraga*, 15–16

About the Author

T. JACKIE CUEVAS is a faculty member at the University of Texas at San Antonio.

Available titles in the Latinidad: Transnational Cultures in the United States series:

María Acosta Cruz, *Dream Nation: Puerto Rican Culture and the Fictions of Independence*

Rodolfo F. Acuña, *The Making of Chicana/o Studies: In the Trenches of Academe*

Xóchitl Bada, *Mexican Hometown Associations in Chicagoacán: From Local to Transnational Civic Engagement*

Adriana Cruz-Manjarrez, *Zapotecs on the Move: Cultural, Social, and Political Processes in Transnational Perspective*

T. Jackie Cuevas, *Post-Borderlandia: Chicana Literature and Gender Variant Critique*

Marivel T. Danielson, *Homecoming Queers: Desire and Difference in Chicana Latina Cultural Production*

Allison E. Fagan, *From the Edge: Chicana/o Border Literature and the Politics of Print*

Jerry González, *In Search of the Mexican Beverly Hills: Latino Suburbanization in Postwar Los Angeles*

Rudy P. Guevarra Jr., *Becoming Mexipino: Multiethnic Identities and Communities in San Diego*

Colin Gunckel, *Mexico on Main Street: Transnational Film Culture in Los Angeles before World War II*

Marie-Theresa Hernández, *The Virgin of Guadalupe and the Conversos: Uncovering Hidden Influences from Spain to Mexico*

Lisa Jarvinen, *The Rise of Spanish-Language Filmmaking: Out from Hollywood's Shadow, 1929–1939*

Regina M. Marchi, *Day of the Dead in the USA: The Migration and Transformation of a Cultural Phenomenon*

Desirée A. Martín, *Borderlands Saints: Secular Sanctity in Chicano/a and Mexican Culture*

Marci R. McMahon, *Domestic Negotiations: Gender, Nation, and Self-Fashioning in US Mexicana and Chicana Literature and Art*

A. Gabriel Meléndez, *Hidden Chicano Cinema: Film Dramas in the Borderlands*

Priscilla Peña Ovalle, *Dance and the Hollywood Latina: Race, Sex, and Stardom*

Amalia Pallares, *Family Activism: Immigrant Struggles and the Politics of Noncitizenship*

Luis F. B. Plascencia, *Disenchanting Citizenship: Mexican Migrants and the Boundaries of Belonging*

Cecilia M. Rivas, *Salvadoran Imaginaries: Mediated Identities and Cultures of Consumption*

Jayson Gonzales Sae-Saue, *Southwest Asia: The Transpacific Geographies of Chicana/o Literature*

Mario Jimenez Sifuentez, *Of Forest and Fields: Mexican Labor in the Pacific Northwest*

Maya Socolovsky, *Troubling Nationhood in U.S. Latina Literature: Explorations of Place and Belonging*

Susan Thananopavarn, *LatinAsian Cartographies: History, Writing, and the National Imaginary*

Printed in the United States
By Bookmasters